SECRET
NORTHAMPTONSHIRE

SECRET
NORTHAMPTONSHIRE

PETER HILL

AMBERLEY

Dr Peter Hill is a lecturer in higher education and adult life-long learning. In September 2005 he was presented with an award at the Guildhall in Northampton for Services to Local History in Northamptonshire.

He is the author of seventeen books, including 'Folklore of Northamptonshire' which was shortlisted for the prestigious Kathleen Briggs Award in 2006 for the best publication in folklore.

First published 2009

Amberley Publishing Plc
Cirencester Road, Chalford,
Stroud, Gloucestershire, GL6 8PE

www.amberleybooks.com

British Library Cataloguing in Publication Data.
A catalogue record for this book is available from the British Library.

ISBN 978 1 84868 720 2
Typesetting and Origination byAmberley Publishing
Printed in Great Britain

CONTENTS

ACKNOWLEDGEMENTS

Such an exhaustive and diverse range of material as a book of this nature requires, involves much research and tracking down. I am grateful, therefore, to the many contacts who have helped in some way with the task of retrieval. Occasionally, this has necessitated asking some of those individuals to carry out a seemingly impossible or time-consuming mission!

I wish to thank Sarah Bridges and other archivists, past and present, at the Northamptonshire Record Office for allowing access to, and usage of, certain items over the years, and also staff at the record offices of Leicestershire and Cambridgeshire. The sources at the National Archives, British Library, specialist material at the libraries of the Law Society, University of Nottingham and English Place Name Society have all been of great use.

Local help has been forthcoming from staff in the county libraries in Northampton (Local Studies Collection), Corby, Oundle, Towcester, Brackley, Daventry, and especially Andrea Pettingale at Kettering Library, who with her great interest in this kind of subject matter has been of enormous assistance and has never complained about the extra work involved whilst carrying out her normal duties. The museums in Northampton, Kettering and Oundle have also played a small part, as have the heritage centres in Rothwell and Desborough.

A special mention must be given to those individuals who provided additional information and material, namely Brian Andrews, Burl Bellamy, Quentin Bland, John Clarke, David and Elizabeth Close, Frank Ellis, Lil Evans, Glenn Foard, Maurice Goodwin, Elsie Harrison, Carl Hector, Hilary Hillman, Elizabeth Jordan, Bob Mears, Tracey Partida, David Pain, David Palmer, Sue Payne, Elvin Royall, Chris Royall, Beryl Simon and Reg Sutton.

A rewarding, fortuitous experience has been lecturing to local history societies, specialist interest groups, the U3A and the WI, and running courses for the WEA around the county on themes and subject matter, a great deal of which has been relevant to this book. Two positive outcomes of this were, firstly, seeing the enthusiasm and interest shown by many of those attending, some of whom wanted to explore a certain topic further, either through general interest or for more academic reasons, for which I was able to provide additional sources and resources as a starting point. Secondly, I was able to gain familiarity and a better insight into the local history and heritage of each specific locality, from information given to me by various individuals at these sessions through conversation, correspondence or donated material. In other words all these activities have been a two-way process. Therefore, I am extremely grateful for each contribution they have made, however small.

Finally a word of sincere thanks to Sarah Slight of Amberley Publishing for her interest shown in the subject matter, and getting this work into print form for a wider readership to enjoy.

INTRODUCTION

Northamptonshire of all the shires
The most the poets' soul inspires
For springs, abundant spires
For spinsters fair, and haughty squires

Few people would have disagreed with this rhyme, current throughout the county during the 1800s but now long since forgotten. It is indeed a unique county in many respects. Virtually in the centre of England, its elongated shape sprawling in a northeast-southwest orientation, it is surrounded by eight other shires (more than any other county): Leicestershire, Warwickshire, Oxfordshire, Rutland, Cambridgeshire, Lincolnshire, Bedfordshire and Buckinghamshire, all of which have had some linguistic and cultural influence.

Historically, it was also affected by being divided into two parts, the upper portion for some years under the Danelaw (created in the ninth century), hence a Scandinavian influence, and the lower, smaller portion south of Watling Street (now the A5), under Anglo-Saxon administration. This division also helped to shape the character of the county, especially in some of its vocabulary.

Yet in spite of what it has absorbed, the county has developed its own identity and peculiarities (such as a one-time superstition that bad luck would befall anyone baking on Good Friday).

It has witnessed several important and pivotal events in the history of the nation, and has been the home of men and women of literary, scientific, religious and antiquarian acclaim, some of whom went on attain national and international importance.

But there is another side to the county's heritage, for tucked away in all kinds of places is a treasure trove of items of interest, either forgotten, lost or hidden (some accidentally, others by time and circumstance). They can be found in a vast range of places: documents, records, deeds, letters, diaries and journals, antiquarian books and pamphlets, posters, old newspapers and magazines, maps, photos, postcards and even artefacts. In addition conversation and interviews (recorded or remembered) with people in the twilight years of their lives, those links with a vanishing or vanished era, have something of precious value. Much could have otherwise have been lost, as indeed much has, seemingly too insignificant or commonplace to record such as everyday life, village characters and happenings in a community, or events of some importance at the time but which have somehow been forgotten in the mists of time.

Let us take another step forward now and look at the foundations of local history in the county, for therein amongst the facts, dates and well-known topics, are some things that are only lightly touched on or hinted at in some way, whilst other things are missing or awaiting further discovery even now.

Perhaps the first county historian was Sir Thomas Brudenell (1578-1663) of Deene Park who collected items of local interest in the area, together with his good friend Christopher Hatton III (c. 1605-1670) of Kirby Hall. They were also acquainted with the pioneering historians, William Dugdale and Roger Dodsworth who together visited the two local men on several occasions, exchanging information and ideas, and sharing expertise. Unfortunately, during the Civil War, disgruntled Parliamentarian troops came to Deene Park and ransacked the home of the absent Royalist, Sir Thomas, burning, discarding and pilfering papers, books and furnishings. We cannot imagine how much, if anything, of local historical importance was lost. Whatever the situation, in the following century John Bridges made use of Brudenell's material for the first book on the history of Northamptonshire (published several years after his death, in 1771). In his task he was ably provided with relevant material by other scholars around the county, among them John Morton (1671-1726), rector of Great Oxendon, who had earlier published 'The Natural History of Northamptonshire' in 1712. Both of these authors' books contain useful references to names, places and features of the county, often giving a tantalising glimpse of something not found before or since, thereby providing us with a valuable record – and a starting point for further investigation.

Another visitor to the county at that time was the great William Stukeley (1687-1765), rector of All Saints' church, Stamford, a member of the Society of Antiquaries and Fellow of the Royal Society, and author on ancient monuments, whose good friend was John Montagu of Boughton House, whom he visited several times. The building and grounds interested him greatly and he made copious notes during his visits, on one occasion designing a bridge for the park. On one of his 'itineraries', whilst passing through the county with companions via Fotheringhay and Oundle, he mentioned 'the excellent ale to be had' in Geddington and described the newly constructed buildings in Northampton, still recovering from the great fire of the previous century.

Yet another visitor was Horace Walpole (1717-1797), youngest son of the first British prime minister, and a major figure in the Gothic Revival, who wrote the first novel of that genre, *The Castle of Otranto*, and was builder of the extraordinary Strawberry Hill. He wrote flatteringly about Drayton House at Lowick, but advised travellers not to stay in Wellingborough!

That same century saw the printing of the first newspaper in the county, the *Northampton Mercury*, in 1720, and on the periphery, the earlier Stamford Mercury, 1714. Both publications contained nuggets of information regarding local news, events, advertisements, and other features of county life, just like today's newspapers, albeit in a different style and form. The founder of the Northampton Mercury, William Dicey, also printed chapbooks, calendars, maps and games, which were sold at his printing works/shop in Northampton and at Bow in London. Successive members of his family continued as proprietors of the newspaper until the middle of the next century.

Meanwhile, national periodical *The Gentleman's Magazine* (1731-1907) was first published. Although with a countrywide distribution and published in London, there were often items about Northamptonshire in its pages, some not always mentioned in the county's publications.

Two artists made significant contributions towards how the landscape and buildings looked at the time they were working. Peter Tillemans (1684-1734), made several drawings for John Bridges of locations being covered for his history of the county. In the next century, George Clarke of Scaldwell (1790-1868) drew a massive 17,000 sketches, mainly of churches and manor houses, whilst making frequent journeys around Northamptonshire and other counties in the process.

The nineteenth century was to be a watershed in the documentation of the county's local history, especially with reference to some of its more quirky or unusual items. In 1849 a new weekly publication, *Notes and Queries*, appeared in Oxford, the brainchild of an academic, William Thomas (1802-1885), who also first coined the term 'folklore'. Readers, whatever their background, were invited to contribute items of historical and literary interest. The publication struck a chord and began to appear in local versions around the nation, with the first Northamptonshire *Notes and Queries* being published in 1884 and running until 1895, under three successive editors, W.D. Sweeting, John Taylor and Christopher Markham, the latter starting up and editing a new series after a ten year hiatus, from 1905 until 1927. He also published an important series of books and papers on various aspects of the county from church features to local village sayings, which continued until his death in 1937.

The aforementioned John Taylor (1831-1901) was a bibliophile, collector, printer and bookseller who set up the Dryden Press in College Street, Northampton, where he started up a trade in old publications, and reprinting many rare books and pamphlets mainly about the county. His mission was to collect every scrap of Northamptonshire's history and produce 'a complete bibliography of every book written and printed by a county man', scrupulously making careful notes about each item.

The 1800s also saw the emergence of a remarkable group of clergy antiquarians and scholars, who all made significant contributions to the county's history. Firstly, William Kaye Bonney (1780-1862), rector of Kingscliffe, who wrote *Historical Notes with Reference to Fotheringhay* (1824), the intruiging and somewhat scarce *The Forest Legend*, and a valuable unpublished manuscript on the history of Kingscliffe, all of which contained previously undocumented historical information. Robert Meyrick Serjeantson (1861-1916), rector of St Peter's, Northampton, wrote about an aspect of his church, co-authored a history of the nearby Church of the Holy Sepulchre (1897), and was joint editor of the first two volumes of the Victoria County History of Northamptonshire (1902, 1906). His friend, the formidable Henry Isham Longden, (1859-1942), rector of Heyford, painstakingly researched and gleaned valuable information from various archives throughout his long life, two of his works being the mammoth (fifteen volume) *Northamptonshire and Rutland Clergy from 1500* (published 1938-1943, with addenda and an index added in 1952), and a pioneering work co-authored with Serjeantson on the parish churches and religious houses of the county (1913). The final member of the trio was John Charles Cox (1843-1919), rector of Holdenby, who was on the Central Committee of the Victoria County History, and also added his own contribution as author of several books, including another book on the parish churches of the county 'illustrated by parishioners wills, temp. Henry VIII' (1901).

To this cluster of antiquarians, we must add John Askham (1825-1894), a Wellingborough shoemaker and poet who also wrote *Sketches in Prose and Verse* giving a glimpse of his early life in the area when life was simpler, before the great changes sweeping the county during the course of the century. Finally, Charles Wise (1825-1910), a Warkton schoolmaster, who produced five books, one on Rockingham Castle and the forest area (1891), and another *The Montagus of Boughton and their Northamptonshire Homes* (1888).

The mid-twentieth century built on these strong foundations, with many useful features of local interest appearing in six volumes of *Northamptonshire County Magazine* (1928-1933). However, it was the formation in 1920 of the Northamptonshire Record Society by Joan Wake which was the crowning achievement of all that had gone before. She worked tirelessly collecting and preserving priceless manuscripts, documents and maps, with the aim of finding a secure central place of storage. This ambition was realised when, after moving from different locations, the archives she had created were housed in a new purpose-built home at Wootton Hall.

The society's purpose was to give lectures on aspects of local history and to study the material she had amassed. It was a great success and led to the first issue (1948) of an annual publication, *Northamptonshire Past and Present*, which flourishes today. Thereafter, local history societies sprang up around the county, some eventually producing their own magazine, whilst *Northamptonshire Local History News*, a quarterly publication which contained interesting contributions from county enthusiasts, enabled the societies to advertise their programme of speakers. Many of them joined the Northamptonshire Association for Local History on its foundation in January 1995, which now has an annual History Day, and since 2001, has printed *Hindsight* magazine, the successor to *NHLS*.

So ends this tour through the ages of how the rich heritage of the county's history has been created. Let us now have a look at some of the more 'secret' aspects of the county's history, both within various archives and what can be traced outside in the villages and countryside.

I-SPY

'Get out and about, and not just bury your noses in documents.'
W.G. Hoskins

Many of us fondly remember playing I-Spy as children and even buying the little *6d* or *1s* books of that name, covering a range of subjects that made us look out for all kinds of things that helped us score points – the rarer the object, the higher the score. It was a real 'voyage of discovery', arousing our curiosity and increasing our knowledge about the world around us.

We can apply those same 'skills' today when scouring the streets and countryside of the county, for although much of the past has been destroyed or altered, sometimes beyond recognition, some things from a bygone era are still there, maybe rusting or peeling, hidden in grass, covered with foliage, encrusted with moss or lichen or faint marks on walls or other structures. These are just some examples.

In the small village of Wakerley there are an amazing number of such features. At different ends of the street, there are two small enamel signs that have somehow managed to survive the ravages of time, dating from the Second World War: one can be found on the wall of a house where the village air-raid warden lived, the other on a wooden building where the first-aid facility was housed. Near the latter, in a neighbouring field, stand four unique circular structures with concrete bases. Two of these have a brick-built upper 'storey'. They date from another wartime period, the First World War, and were built by prisoners of war, though the structures were never completed – or used. They were intended to be calcining kilns for refining iron-ore from the nearby quarries: the process was used to prepare ore for smelting by burning limestone to remove the impurities. At the other end of the village where the road crosses the Welland into Rutland is a fine bridge, of fourteenth-century origin, which was repaired in 1793. On either side of

The air raid warden's sign on a house at Wakerley.

the parapet, overlooking the river and protruding from the wall, there is a stone head, originally marking the boundary with Rutland. The parapet itself is not without interest, covered at one end with deeply incised initials, names and dates. Some are for amusement but others commemorate a great flood, one line reading 'FLOOD.JULY.1868'. Recording such an event was not unusual, for example on the wall of the old millhouse at Bulwick is engraved 'BF 1711' (the letters denoting the name of someone involved in some way at the time). It is worth seeking out others around the county, especially on old bridges (even at water level), but they do not make themselves readily known!

It was also common practice to engrave graffiti on other structures, such as the walls of dwellings, where they are readily identifiable, and even on the great houses (a good example being those carved by nineteenth and early twentieth-century visitors on the outer walls of the forecourt of Kirby Hall). But there are also a considerable number on church walls, some done to pass the time by local lads (an early example of vandalism?), some by zealous churchwardens or priests, and in some cases by prisoners from the Napoleonic Wars involved in some form of work on the buildings, two examples being a group of inscriptions on the south side of the Church of St Peter and St Paul in Kettering and, more intriguingly, according to village tradition – but less verifiable – unknown coats of arms on the inner window sills of the church at Wilbarston. Graffiti was also quite commonplace on the wooden stalls and pews of churches in the eighteenth and nineteenth centuries, as at Easton on the Hill and East Carlton. They can usually be found at or near the rear of the church, where boys, or even their fathers, possibly out of boredom during a sermon, would carve them with less chance of being seen! At Oundle can be found graffiti and doodles on the screen separating the south chapel from the chancel – again, out of view from the minister.

Graffiti and inscriptions can also appear in the most unlikely places, both externally and internally. At Stoke Bruerne on part of the wall of the extended enclosure on the west side of the churchyard is an enigmatic inscribed tablet, with spaced lettering: 'A 1893 D, P NG E, W NG E, C KM E, S EP D, G S D T Q, T O O G', which has been plausibly deciphered (though not verified) as: 'Parson Gave, Warden Drove, Clerk Made, Squire Paid, God Save The Queen, To Our Own God'. This certainly seems in accord with the roles of various officials and the lord of the manor in parish matters, especially in an age of great church restoration, institutional reorganisation and paternalism. Religious fervour extended to the interior fabric of some of the older houses in the county.

On a beam above the parlour at Manor Farm at Wadenhoe is the inscription 'Jehovah' and '1593'. Strangely they are *inverted*, a superstitious device perhaps to ward off evil attempting to enter the house – a practice not completely unknown during that time of religious upheaval. On a bressumer above the wide fireplace of an early seventeenth-century house in West Street, Kingscliffe, there is a long rambling two-verse diatribe of eighty-two words in black lettering on a painted background, that begins 'As hatrid is the (Christia)ns, so friendshippe is the loving gifte of God. The druncken friend is a friend very evill...the franticke friend is for the devil. The quiet friend all one word and diede...' On the wooden surrounds of a large fireplace in a house at Hall Hill in Brigstock is a similar religious verse.

The most mysterious inscription, however, was found on an oak mantelpiece at Helmdon in the latter years of the nineteenth century. It depicts a dragon with a foliate tail and the lettering 'Mo Dom Ano 133' (the latter having a missing digit following the inferred 'year', making it either 1133 or 1233. There is also a possibility of a later date, but the image of the foliate dragon concords with the earlier dates here, being a fashionable motif in religious houses during the Norman, Transitional and Early English periods of architectural design. If this is so, however, there is something out of place, for only Roman numerals existed at that time in Britain (and Europe) – Arabic numerals were not in use until the mid-fifteenth century and only became widely used with the invention of the printing press.

It is commonplace today to find old buildings that have since been converted into homes like buildings that were once used for other purposes, such as barns, granaries, shops, hostelries, or workshops such as blacksmith's forge. Again, apart from visual identification – references in trade directories and other records, or a name plate on the wall of a house signifying its former function or existence, such as 'The Old Post Office' or 'The Red Lion'– there are other tell-tale signs of its past, such as the horse-tethering ring of a village smithy, a wooden 'arm' jutting out from the upper part of a wall above a small opening or doorway, signifying a granary, a wooden post (or again a wooden arm) that once held a hostelry sign, triangular vents in the walls (a former barn) and so on. More unusual features are reminders of an occupation that was to die out by the 1950s, as the car replaced the horse as the normal means of transportation: a huge horseshoe displayed on the gable end of the former forge, which stands alongside the Stamford road in Collyweston, and an anvil embedded in the wall of the forge that operated at Milton Malsor. Equally as rare are enamel trade or advertising plaques. Once common, their golden era being from 1880 until 1950, the majority have disappeared, victims of social change like so many other features of the streets and countryside. One survivor is at Mears Ashby where the rusting enamel sign of a former farrier can be seen, seemingly defying time on the wall of the old premises. Circular yellow AA signs giving distances between towns can also still be found, one at Kingscliffe on the wall of the former Red Lion public house and the other at Collyweston, which has been re-sited a few metres away from the A43, in the yard of the village museum.

Another rare survival is the milestone, a one-time necessary feature along the major routes of the realm, although not too common until the coaching era, after the Turnpike Acts of 1744 and 1766 had made them compulsory. It is a rewarding experience to come across one, as so many have been uprooted and discarded anonymously. Where they do occur, however, they have gained a form of protection in being listed. Uniquely, three survivals lie in close proximity in the north of the county. One can be found at Thrapston, on the old road to Oundle, close to a modern service-station. This fine relic of the past reflects the importance of livestock markets in the olden days, with the inscription on one side '9 Furlongs To Thrapston Cattle Market' and on the other, 'To Oundle 7 Miles'. A second milestone, dating from the early nineteenth century, can be found just outside Oundle (in Ashton parish) on the west side of the A605, where it was partially re-sited when road widening took place a few years ago. It is inscribed 'To Peterborough 12 Miles, To

A rare survival of an occupational sign at Mears Ashby.

Oundle 1 Mile'. The third of the trio is the most unusual of all and can be found at Oundle. Countless people, in particular those living in the town, have walked past it, unaware of its existence, for it is almost unrecognisable, embedded in the upper section of the boundary wall of the churchyard, depicting hands with fingers pointing in two directions and the lettering 'To Peterboro 13 Miles, To Thrapston-Cross 7¾'. On the Grand Union Canal at Gayton there is a cast iron milepost giving the distance to Northampton as 5 miles, and to Braunston as 16¾.

Erected for a similar purpose, but more common in their modern form (both in design and fabric) were fingerposts, or waymarkers. Almost statutory from 1697 when magistrates were empowered to have them erected at 'cross highways', the situation remained almost unchanged until the 1964 Traffic Act which, although not compulsory, regulated the system we still have today with some form of national uniformity and standardisation. Survivors do exist – more numerous than milestones – and those in the county are usually painted green with white lettering (albeit stencilled in plastic or metal), the board being attached to a white wooden post, or in some cases a replacement reinforced

The unique 'Six Ways' fingerpost high up on a hill overlooking several villages.

concrete post. Good examples can be found at Bears Lane, just outside Weldon, marking an ancient track to Brigstock and, in better condition, just outside Wadenhoe on the Aldwincle-Pilton road at the head of the old cattle drover's track, with the lettering 'Bridle and Drift Road To Lowick. No Through Road For Vehicles'– a reminder of a time before the car disrupted and dominated a centuries-old slower, more peaceful way of life.

Most unique of all fingerposts, however, is a set of six known as Six Ways, standing in glorious isolation, at the top of a steep slope overlooking the village of Ashley in the distance on one side, and with a commanding aspect of neighbouring Brampton Ash, Weston by Welland and Sutton Bassett. These appear to have been almost forgotten by time, consisting of six 'fingers' with hand-painted lettering on a green background, pointing in different directions to each of the aforementioned settlements. It is well worth the steep climb not just to see them but to take in the panoramic views.

Parish boundary markers are a similar rarity. Cast-iron examples can be found around the county, examples being at the adjoining settlements of Cottingham and Middleton, and on the bridge over the River Welland at Duddington, marking the boundary with neighbouring Tixover. Another

*The medieval stone cross marking
the parish boundaries between
Blatherwycke and Kings Cliffe.*

lies along the Harborough road between Brampton Ash and Dingley and is inscribed 'Parish Boundary, Brampton, Dingley'.

A more unusual form of boundary marker can be found at Oundle, on South Bridge, one of the three bridges over the River Nene in that town. Highly visible on the parapet are the deeply-incised capital letters B and O separated by a large vertical line, denoting Barnwell and Oundle. Another equally unusual parish boundary marker, can be found low down almost at water level on the bridge over the River Ise at Warkton, denoting the division between that village and neighbouring Kettering. Even more unique is a rare survival of a medieval cross, White Cross, which marks the boundary between Blatherwycke and Kingscliffe, and can be seen standing by a tree close to the road, though it is sometimes obscured from view by greenery. It has a distinctive design, with short side arms and a wheel head cross finial.

Its contemporaries have been less fortunate, lost in the mists of time, with only references in records as to their existence – names like Gibbescrosse (near Duddington), Huxloe Cross (near Lowick) and White Cross, examples of the latter being at or near Fotheringhay, Weekley, and Pipewell. A recent tragic loss was that of the boundary stone along the road from Corby to Cottingham, where it had stood since at least the eighteenth century. It was inscribed with a key on one side (for Corby, whose parish church was dedicated to St Peter) and a cross on the other (for Cottingham). It was removed when road widening was being carried out and supposedly placed for safekeeping at an unknown location. Regrettably, it has not been seen since and is believed to have been demolished when building development took place. The area in which it had stood was where four parishes formerly had grazing rights, and there was once a reference to this and the stone in a local rhyme: 'Oakley O, Gretton G, Cottingham Cross and Corby Key'.

Parish boundaries, of course, were of vital importance to a community, which needed divine benevolence in the form of good weather and a successful harvest – basically for survival – and Rogation Day (during Ascension Week) was an occasion when those boundaries were inspected and reaffirmed by male members of the community. They would stop at each boundary marker or limit, where the bounds would be struck with a stripped willow branch, led by the curate who would admonish the crowd not to transgress on neighbouring boundaries and 'remove their landmarks' and exhort them to give thanks and praise the earth for the bounty it provided – the purer the conscience and the holier the thoughts, the better the prospects would be in the coming year. The litany and two psalms would also be read during the perambulation.

Known as 'Beating the Bounds' it could be quite a violent and traumatic occasion for those participating for the first time, especially boys who would suffer at certain boundary points by having their heads 'lightly' knocked against a boundary tree or stone, or be thrown into a ditch, so that they would remember and uphold the all-important limits of the parish, thereby safeguarding against possible future encroachment by an adjoining parish. However, what was also appealing was that sustenance was provided by the church (and in some cases by disgruntled wealthier residents who objected to wasting money on their drunk and disorderly neighbours!). Churchwarden's accounts often give a good example of what was provided and the expense involved. For example, at Towcester in June 1720, there is an entry:

in ye morn: Ale and Bread 1/9; At offle Meadow Plank: 24 qts Ale, 3 Doz. Bread 11/-; at High Hay 16 qts, 7 penny loaves, 5/11; At night when came home: 23 qts Ale 7/8, for supper: A leg of Mutton and Veale Pye, 4/-

This was obviously hard work!

Occasionally, details of such a perambulation would be recorded in parish registers. This would depend on the interest or importance attached to such a commonplace occasion by the current incumbent or curate of the parish church. One notable example was that of John Cable of the Church of St Michael at Great Oakley, who gave a remarkably detailed description of that which took place in 1616, interestingly not during Ascension week, but on 28 November, by 'inhabitants of Okley in the manner following':

> At a Gapp at the corner of Severick leas (they) kept to a baulk in banks which leadeth into a cross in Myll Field adjacent to hear (sic)...and kept on to Crabb Tree Baulk and soe went thorow a gap wher there is a quick ledge..till they came against the Grange house. and went thorow a Garden Place..into the lanes.. over a bridge..came to Bailies Bowke full of Thornes..came beneath Longfield Pond...over a hedge into Swynhoe, up a Ryding.. sett their Mark and left Lawnd Railes....came to a water hollow..down the valley into CalderMeddow Lodge and came to the top of Shewtors Hill and so retourned into Okely.

Normally such an occasion would take most of the day, carried out at a leisurely pace. However, there could be exceptions if the May weather was unseasonably bad. The Oundle carpenter, John Clifton, noted in his diary for 6 May, 1782:

> A severe day, cold wet and uncomfortable this morning, but there were about 100 horsemen and Boys went round the Bounds, they rode as if the Devil was in them...

Field names often reflected where disputed boundaries existed, and there are several all round Northamptonshire, showing what a quarrelsome county it was! These names contained some form of the prefix 'flit', an Old English word for a dispute, and there are examples at Yelvertoft, Cottesbrooke, Harpole, Clipston, Passenham, Gayton, Harlestone, Benefield, Easton on the Hill, Isham, Boughton, Braybrooke and Irtlingborough – to name just a few! Other names show where a boundary was situated, such as 'Mere' at Harpole, Mardale at Braunston, Landymore at Spratton, and Laundimer Woods at Brigstock (both from Old English 'gemaere' – a boundary) and Sharrow (Old English 'scearu' – boundary) at Harlestone which marked the division between the East and West Fields, or where four boundaries met as was the case for Twywell, Islip, Woodford and Lowick (in field names prefixed with variations of the Middle English word 'alange', meaning remote). At Wicken, a kind of boundary-marking occasion, took place to celebrate the reuniting of the two parishes Wykedyve and Wykehamon in 1587, and it is still celebrated under a (younger) elm tree with the reading of Psalm 100 (the Gospel Elm Ceremony) in Ascension Week, followed by the consumption of cakes and ale. A huge spiced cake (in some respects a form of marking new boundaries) is specially made for the occasion.

The name still survives at a sharp bend in the road between Southwick and Bulwick Leys (an extra-parochial area), where Crossway Hand Lodge stands (the area was known in 1704 as 'Cross-a-hand') and it was once the name of an area at Higham Ferrers (Handcross Fields).

Occasionally one finds a large boulder of a stone not native to the area, usually of granite or quartzite. This is likely to be a 'glacial erratic', a stone deposited during the upheaval of the Ice Age, rather than something transported by human means from another place. Where they occured – either in a field (as at East Farndon), or in a street (as at Gretton) – they were regarded with wonder by our ancestors from prehistoric times to as late as the early nineteenth century, and treated as special 'hallowed' places for the conducting of judicial matters such as settling disputes, business dealings, speeches, or other matters where an oath, agreement or promise of some kind was made – something to be honoured. Later they would just be seen as curiosities or even used for other purposes, that at Geddington, close to the Eleanor Cross, was said to have been used as a block for mounting horses! Some have been named – usually with variations in spelling of the Old English word 'haran' (grey) – and these often acted as boundary markers such as at Horestone Meadow/Horse Stone Brook, separating Nether Heyford from Bugbrooke, and Whorestone Furlong at Desborough.

The great houses of the county, past and present, had a variety of outbuildings and other structures that have long since ceased to function in the capacity for which they were constructed. Some of these have been converted to other, more modern uses. Others, however, have long been abandoned or fallen into decay, yet they still stand, often in glorious isolation, and in some instances outlasting the old manor house they served, such as the eighteenth-century stable block at Blatherwycke, tucked away by itself at the back of the village church. Hidden away high up on a wall is the coat of arms of Donatus O'Brien, depicting a hand brandishing a sword and the date, 1770. The old manor house itself was demolished in 1948, apparently after the last in line of the manorial family, two unmarried sisters, stated that since only *their* family had lived continuously in the building (and its predecessor) for several generations, that no one else should live in it after their demise.

A 'glacial erratic' at Geddington. This would have been a sacred feature in ancient times.

Other manorial survivals include icehouses. Originally an eighteenth-century innovation for keeping food fresh, they stored ice cut in slabs from a nearby pond or lake during the winter which was then laid on straw bedding within an underground chamber. They were gradually outmoded from the middle of the following century by early forms of the refrigerator. Often dome-shaped and camouflaged by nature and time with a covering of foliage or moss, they can be found, now sealed up, some distance from the house, such as those at Aynho and Bulwick. In the grounds of Glendon Hall near Kettering, one nineteenth-century example underwent an amazing transformation after it had gone out of use, with a hipped-roof privy being built over it, with three large seats and two smaller ones!

Dovecotes (sometimes known as columbariums) are, of course, common and once provided a useful variety of resources (initially) for manorial and religious houses and later for farmhouses, including meat and even eggs for food, feathers for bedding and guano for fertiliser, as well as acting as messengers on occasions. The shape of the building, whether circular, square or rectangular, was a matter of preference, not necessarily one of fashion. Circular types appear to have been more common in Northamptonshire from the eighteenth century, and were more practical, allowing better access to the roosting boxes and ledges, with the aid of a 'potence' – a rotating central wooden pole with a ladder. There is also a rare octagonal example at Charlton in the south of the county.

Seven circular types are known to still exist, some with the original 'glovers' (roof openings): Apethorpe (with domed roof and lantern, later converted into a water tower), Eaglethorpe, Kingscliffe (with lantern), Denton, Bulwick, Cranford St Andrew and Wadenhoe – the latter two are available for public access. However, the most spectacular dovecote lies in isolation in a field at Newton near Geddington, where the former manor house of a branch of the Tresham family once stood. It is of immense size, rectangular in plan and has a dividing wall within. Access is via two low doorways at either end, one of which still has part of an original oak door. Engraved on a stone tablet at the top of the front elevation is the name MAURICE TRESHAM.

Of particular interest are the vestiges of former dovecotes. Many of these can be seen at the gable ends of cottages, or outbuildings now converted into dwellings, and consist of one remaining wall of nesting boxes. Although exposed to the elements some of these are still actually used, as at Geddington (Dove Farm), charmingly occupied by white doves. At Wilbarston, adjoining the garden wall of Pilgrim Cottage (The Old House) and now facing a school field, is one side of what was a large square dovecote.

Rarer still are bathhouses. In a swathe of trees, at the far end of the grounds of Rushton Hall, stands St Peter's Spring Bath House, an ornate structure dating mainly from the mid nineteenth century. Formerly with a glazed roof, it suffered from the ravages of time and was left open to the elements for many years. It was sympathetically restored in January 2000, with the walls cleaned up and cleared of greenery. Dating mainly from the nineteenth century, it has both external and internal niches, some with Latin inscriptions on stone tablets above, and one over the mouth of the spring. Another larger niche, situated inside and opposite the entrance, contains the effigy of a recumbent female figure and an inscription, which translated means:

Nymph of the spot, this sacred font I keep, And by the murmur of its waters sleep. My slumber spare, who seekest this marble cave, And drink in silence, or in silence lave.

There still exists, though long disused, an open spa in the parish of Southwick, tucked away in a field above Kings Cliffe. It was first exploited in 1670 and soon became a popular destination for those afflicted with various ailments, for bathing in its chalybeate water (it was even used to make tea!). It consists of one large rectangular brick-lined tank with a small set of access steps and an

A rare surviving wall of a rectangular 'columbarium' at Wilbarston.

adjoining smaller chamber. Engraved on the walls are names and dates, varying from 1747 to the end of the nineteenth century. The iron-rich water still bubbles up occasionally. Similar celebrated seventeenth-century spas existed at King's Sutton, Astrop (St Rumbold's Well) and Wellingborough, visited by Charles I, which at one time was said to have as many as thirty-five wells, the water also being used to make mineral waters and stout by local brewer, Dulley and Woolston in the nineteenth century. Some of this water, after the brewing process was completed, was channelled into a specially-created bathing area for the townsfolk. A section of this is now on display at the newly-opened heritage centre.

With such a well-watered county, it is only natural that many of its springs were used for drawing water, as the many wellheads and pumps testify, some with date stones still intact, if a little eroded. Excellent examples can be found around the streets of the joint settlements of Cottingham-Middleton. Some of the pumps have a more ornate appearance, such as the nineteenth-century pair standing close together at the top end of Church Lane in Dingley, close to the Harborough Road. One is encased in a cast-iron 'jacket' and has a decorated spout; its companion has a lion motif on the column. Both still have their original handles.

There are also two interesting instances where a pump has been re-sited. At Fotheringhay in the spring of 2000, the old village pump was rediscovered,

The eighteenth-century bathhouse adjoining St Peter's Spring in the grounds of Rushton Hall.

lying amongst a large clump of overgrown bushes near the stone wall adjacent to the ancient Garden House (a former inn connected with the royal York family in medieval times). It has a lead cistern with rose motifs, and much of the remaining fabric, including some oak casing, was virtually intact. It was consequently restored and now resides in close proximity to where it was found, in a recess where it can be viewed from the street. Its lead butts, dated 1643, are displayed in the church.

At Ashley, along the main street, there is a well-preserved pump and its attached handle, standing within a wooden frame. Its original location was in the 'Town Yard', to the east of where the village hall now stands. From there it served ten dwellings which, it is said, could accommodate up to a hundred people, possibly basket-makers who made use of the large number of osiers along the main road. Today, the pump is the only survivor from the 'Town Yard'.

Not so common, however, are well houses. One can be found in the grounds of Fermyn Woods Hall near Brigstock. It was erected at the behest of two sisters, the Ladies Fitzpatrick, in 1828. It is octagonal in plan with a domed

Two of the remaining water pumps at Dingley.

head, fish-scale decorated panels, gargoyles at the corners, a lionhead spout, an iron pump handle at the rear, and a rectangular stone basin at the foot of the structure.

The earliest means of crossing a river on foot would have been via a ford, a log, or stepping stones. Later examples of the latter could still be found until very recently, for example over the River Nene at Nassington. Another primitive means would have been a clam bridge – a single slab of stone spanning the water. These are unknown in the county, but there are still three examples of the more substantial clapper bridge, where two or more slabs are supported by a central pillar or a set of pillars. These can be found at Bugbrooke, Kingscliffe and Wilbarston, the latter on the boundary with Stoke Albany. This bridge, like the others, has obviously had to be repaired or partially replaced over the centuries, but has recently undergone a dramatic transformation during modernisation. That at Kings Cliffe, however, fared much better during renovation in 1999, with new slabs being laid on the brick supports, and the 'original' limestone slabs embedded in adjacent grass verges. It was renamed Leycesters Bridge after one of the villagers who had died at sea five years earlier. The bridge is where an annual duck race takes place every

August Bank Holiday, and was started in 1997 as a fund-raising activity for the community.

Few of the county's medieval bridges remain in their original state or appearance, but one notable exception is the small packhorse bridge at Charwelton, lying on dry ground alongside the main road. Built with ironstone in the fifteenth century to take horses laden with goods over the River Cherwell, it is the only one of this type of bridge in Northamptonshire. It has two pointed arches, a low parapet, and, like other packhorse bridges (and clapper bridges), was just wide enough for the animal to negotiate.

Jordan Bridge (also known as Latimer Bridge) at Braybrooke dates from 1402 and takes its name from the River Jordan, a tributary of the Welland. This fascinating name is not ancient, however, as its origin goes back to the nineteenth century when the nearby Baptist church used its water for baptism. Of such stuff are legends made!

Ornamental bridges for the parkland of the great houses can still be seen, a fine example being that at Deene Park, a three-arched structure spanning an ornamental lake created from the Willow Brook in the late-eighteenth century. Others have virtually disappeared, or only existed in design or in model form. An example of the former once straddled a stream at Kirby Hall, an ornate two-arch bridge with balustrades, and pillars engraved with diamond-shape patterning. It was built in the 1590s but had vanished by the end of the following century, after development of the grounds by Christopher Hatton III and his son. However, vestiges of the lower portion are just discernable, if one looks very carefully, under a mound of turf near the former access way to an adjoining field and the main road.

One bridge that never saw the light of day was that designed by the eighteenth-century antiquary William Stukeley on a visit to Boughton House in 1744. It was an ornate structure in the fashionable Gothic style, with ogee-headed entrances, multiple pinnacles and a vaulted interior.

Causeways have always been a useful way of avoiding a stretch of water in a low-lying area liable to flood from an overflowing river or heavy rainfall. These raised trackways from the days when walking was the most common way to get around, can still be found in many parts of the county, though they are barely used nowadays. Although the majority are of little significance, some are worthy of mention, one of which is listed. This is at Church Walk in Weldon, a one-time renowned limestone quarrying area, with equally famous masons. One of them, William Orsbourne [sic], was responsible for this unusually ornate structure with well-laid square-coursed limestone, ashlar copings and two semi-circular arches and a date stone, 1755.

Causeways are also attached to two ancient bridges over the Nene. A three-arch causeway leads to Ditchford Bridge, which has pedestrian recesses and a date stone recording its origin (1330) and repair in 1927. A five-arch causeway is connected with Irthlingborough Old Bridge, which dates from the mid fourteenth century, and has a plaque depicting the cross of St Peter on one side and a date stone recording later work carried out in 1668.

Another, though less impressive structure, lies at the bottom of the road from Harrington in the direction of Thorpe Underwood, adjoining Newbottle Bridge. It is a long multiple-arched brick structure, with three worn inset stone panels, with the wording 'DCM', 'X' and '1748'.

The stocks, of course, were for punishing minor offences, mainly drunkenness or rowdy behaviour. First recorded in 1201 as 'compedibus', most villages would have had a set, either with or without a whipping post that had fittings or shackles to hold the wrists of the offender. Those that survive today replaced earlier structures. Many more once existed as evidenced in street names like Stocks Lane or Stocks Hill. Survivors can be found at Apethorpe, Eydon, Gretton, Sulgrave (all with whipping posts), Aynho, Brixworth, and King's Sutton, and Little Houghton. The stocks and the less common pillory (used for dishonest traders and fraudsters) both fell into disuse shortly after the reforms of Robert Peel in the late 1830s, though there were instances when the stocks were used at a much later date, such as Geddington in 1857, where they stood at the foot of Eleanor Cross and 1858 at Gretton where a drunk and disorderly man was confined for six hours for refusing to pay a fine. There are some people in the county today who say they should be brought back into use once again to deal with local troublemakers! At Corby, however, stocks *are* still used albeit for a more jovial purpose, when they are periodically renovated and painted ready for the traditional Pole Fair which takes place every twenty years. The stocks hold three 'miscreants' who do not pay a toll for entry into the village on the day, but strangely they have only five holes, leading to all kinds of speculation, including one theory that the odd hole is for somebody with one foot!

Sometimes in place of the stocks, or as an additional method of dealing with disorderly behaviour, there was a village lock-up. Often known as 'roundhouses' they have long since disappeared though they are sometimes marked on old maps, such as that in Corby village, where one stood in The Nook. Another existed, together with stocks and whipping post, opposite the church gates at Rushden. Said to have been brick-built with a ball finial on the roof it was pulled down c.1853 and supposedly replaced with a chestnut tree a few years later. There is one known survivor in Northamptonshire and

The eighteenth-century circular lock-up by the village green at Weldon.

this is at Weldon, where it stands beside the old village green. It is a circular structure, dating from the eighteenth century, with a similar appearance to a dovecote but much smaller, with a ball finial to the roof, heavy studded wooden door and ventilation grilles. With the stocks, this would have been an ideal way of dealing with problems that might arise with four hostelries in close proximity and with the four annual fairs and weekly market on the large adjoining green.

They became defunct shortly after 1839, when the County Police Act led to a paid police force and a compulsory police station with secure cells. One can see one of these cells today in the museum at Oundle, which was once part of the town's Bridewell for local offenders.

The seventeenth-century Bocase Stone, situated along a riding some distance from Brigstock, commemorates a large oak tree, blown down by a gale around the time of Charles I. The now-fading inscription reads 'In this plaes grew Bocase Tree'. Over the years, local theories have been put forward as to the origin of the name, varying from 'bow case', stemming from Robin Hood and his men supposedly hiding his weapons in the tree during one close encounter with adversaries; 'buck case', meaning deer skin; a meeting place for local administration or for archery practice as a nearby field is known as The Bowcast whose length, according to local man Carl Hector, is the range of a bearing arrow, one that is discharged at a 45 degree angle and gives the longest possible range; or a corruption of the name Brocas, a family who were hereditary masters of the Royal Buckhounds who frequently met there. Despite varying theories as to the origin of the name, however, it is most likely to have come from the old Norman French 'bocage', meaning a field at the edge of, or adjoining, a wood.

Its isolation also once gave rise to a supernatural tale in which an eighty-three-year-old wayfarer stops to eat his dinner in the vicinity of the Bocase Stone. Presently, he is interrupted by a gentle sound and the appearance of a beautiful woman 'of foreign hue' on horseback. Touching the reins and enchanted by her voice and manner, he is swept up in a feeling of complete exhilaration. They make their way together along the track conversing and enjoying each other's company, but when they come to a brook the horse shies away, and when he looks in the water his wrinkles and beard have vanished and he sees himself as he was in his youth. Then there is blankness. Next morning he is found by people from Oundle, about a mile from that town, as 'a decrepit wight', babbling about the Bocase Stone and the mystery lady 'who had been kind to him'. This supernatural tale has all the standard trappings of fairylore, which depict a fairy queen with a striking appearance, who tends to appear unexpectedly in isolated places to lonely wayfarers whom she tricks and beguiles with her magic powers. Such isolated spots made our ancestors superstitious – places where one would be vulnerable to supernatural influences, whether harmful or disorientating. Significantly, a large swathe of open countryside in the area was known in the Middle Ages as 'Scratland', possibly derived from Old Norse 'skratti', meaning demon.

Another stone, fashioned in the shape of an 'L', stood at the top of a hill close to the parish boundary between Weldon and Benefield for centuries. According to local tradition it was used as a seat to bind miscreants whilst accusations were read out to them, supposedly a form of village justice. Known also as the Witches Chair, or the Weldon Chair, there is one particular (and unlikely) instance where one such young Weldon man, said to have jealously murdered his sweetheart, was condemned to stay bound to the chair, exposed to the elements, starvation and thirst, until he expired. A baker from Benefield is said to have felt sorry for him and gave him bread or pastries, and some water each time he passed by. After a few days, a check was made by delegated villagers, to see how the man was faring – and of course they were astonished to see him full of health and life. They consequently lay hiding in wait nearby on a 'shift' system to find out what was going on, and sure enough the baker was caught carrying out his charitable actions. He was consequently seized and dealt with, whilst the accused man was left to finish his sentence.

During the Second World War, American airmen from nearby Deenethorpe Airfield, attempting to gain better access along the narrow road whilst transporting various military items, are said to have thrown the 'worthless piece of rock' over a hedge into an adjoining field, where it lay until the 1960s, whereupon it disappeared, supposedly kept in a local barn – or so the story goes. Whatever the case, it has not been seen since.

Before the Great Fire of London in 1666, there was no fire brigade to counter such emergencies. Such matters were handled within the community, with everyone helping out with buckets of water or some other means, and in the case of a larger fire, appealing for assistance from neighbouring villages. With insurance only available for shipping at the time, the devastation wreaked by that conflagration led to the need for some form of building protection, which led to the foundation of private fire insurance companies from 1680. The county has certainly witnessed its fair share throughout the centuries, with major destructive fires occurring in Little Houghton (1333), Kingscliffe (1462), Northampton (notably the Great Fire of 1675), Thrapston (1718), Bozeat (1729), Wellingborough (1738), Everdon (1786), Nassington (1794), Higham Ferrers (1882) and countless others, some of which destroyed nearly the whole settlement. Each company had its own distinctive emblem, which, together with a policy number, was stamped on moulded lead or copper 'fire insurance marks'. These were displayed prominently high up on the front wall of the insured property during an emergency, in view of the company's firemen with their horse-drawn or hand-pulled carts, loaded with leather buckets, pumps and firehooks. The vast majority of dwellings would not have been able to afford the necessary premium and so would have been open to misfortune, but even those that did have a fire insurance mark would not be helped by a rival insurance company in the event of a fire. The situation would not change until municipal fire brigades were formed after 1850. A small number of these fire insurance marks have survived, albeit long out of use, and are worth looking out for, with notable examples visible around the older parts of towns of the county in villages such as Weldon, Blatherwycke and Nassington, and on some of the great houses like Boughton House.

Villages would often keep their fire-fighting equipment in a convenient central location, close to a readily available source of water. Some of the buildings still stand, such as that next to the rectory in Hall Yard, bearing the inscription: 'Erected by Subscription, 1813' and at West Wells, Arnhill Road in Gretton, where a set of springs and wells fed water into a cistern inside the fire engine shed. Perhaps more unusual places for storage, however, were churches, as was the case of Holy Trinity at Rothwell, the longest church in the county. At Harringworth and Stanion, a firehook for pulling off the burning thatch from cottages can be seen in the village church.

Old disused railway 'furnishings' have found new homes, such as track plates used as house numbers and station or crossing gates placed at the entrances to the driveway of a house (as at Lowick, and Duddington) with metal strips along the top bar of the frame informing that 'Any Person Forgetting To Shut And Fasten This Gate Is Liable To A Fine Not Exceeding Forty Shillings'.

It is a sobering thought, perhaps, that as time goes on other common, more modern items of 'street furniture' like the traditional red K6 telephone kiosk will also become few and far between. Only 3,000 around the country have listed status with English Heritage, whilst countless others have no protection. In the summer of 2008, British Telecom announced a cost-cutting measure involving the removal of seventy-three payphones in the north of the county, with justified reasoning that mobile phones and e-mails have drastically reduced the usage of the kiosks. Since then, councils have been given the option of acquiring a kiosk at a minimal cost, with the proviso that they take responsibility for its care and upkeep.

Fortunately, at the present time early wall post boxes and pillar-boxes have some degree of protection. There are a surprisingly high number of Victorian wall boxes – albeit in need of renovation – in villages like Pilton, Achurch, Great Oakley, Cottesbrooke and the town of Desborough. Pillar-boxes from the same era, however, are rare – one known example being tucked away along a side street in Kettering. There is a rare Edward VII wall box at North Street in Oundle and a slightly less rare pillar-box from the same era at South Road in the same town. Those dating from later monarchs have obviously fared better.

It is reckoned that about sixty per cent of sundials are to be found on churches. This leaves a substantial number to be found elsewhere, on rectories and secular buildings. Though known from mosaics in Roman Britain, they did not become a widespread feature, in the form we see today, until the seventeenth century, with their greatest popularity in the next hundred years or so. Some were quite ornate, others had cryptic wording. Perhaps the most attractive example is to be found at Weekley, painted on the front wall on the

A sundial with an unusual inscription, shortly before restoration on a house at Collyweston.

former Montagu Almshouses, on a large red-painted background with two dates, 1611 (the date of the foundation of the building) and 1631 (for the sundial). At Collyweston, on a building in the High Street, is a white-painted sundial with the cryptic wording 'I Ray For No Man', the meaning of which has never been deciphered.

In the nineteenth century, an old circular sundial made of sandstone was dug up in a garden at Little Brington, inscribed with the date 1617 and the Washington family coat of arms. It had belonged to Robert Washington, uncle of the Reverend Laurence Washington, who in turn was the father of two emigrants to Virginia that century, ancestors of the first American president.

Most of the county's many one-time windmills have long disappeared. Like other features of the landscape they are victims of a changing world, leaving only vestiges such as millstones that have been re-sited in gardens and driveways. Unable to compete with industrial mills, which had a faster, larger output, they soon fell into disuse and ultimately into ruin. One of the earliest windmills erected in Britain was in Northamptonshire, recorded in the twelfth century, at Pipewell Abbey. There were three types: the post-mill which, as the name implies, was a fragile structure, consisting of a main timber body or cabin which pivoted on a post, block, or wooden legs which enabled it to rotate and face the direction of the wind; the less-common smock mill, which was like a post mill but was more 'developed' in that had a fixed wooden tower with a movable cap on top, containing the sail axle, the body often hexagonal in shape; and the tower mill, the most sturdy of the three types, with a cap and a stone or brick-built body. One of the most spectacular windmills was that at Eye (then in the Soke of Peterborough) which at one time had *eight* sails instead of the usual four. Accidents were not unknown – there are cases where individuals were hit by the force of the rotating sails. In 1845, fifty- seven-year-old Sarah Northen on visiting the post mill at Kettering was killed whilst conversing. At Braunston in the 1880s, a miller's assistant was struck with such force that he was flung into the adjoining churchyard. In 1876, at Easton on the Hill, twenty-year-old 'Miss Stancer' was hit on the head and killed instantly. Today the mill is a rare survivor, standing a little way from the Stamford road, sail-less, its shell swathed in foliage and a haven for wildlife.

But perhaps the most tragic incident at a mill was not an accident. At Great Oakley in 1865, sixteen-year-old George Pain, the son of the miller, was helping his father at the village post mill, as he had done so many times before. He was suddenly taken ill, and died a few days later. His grief-stricken father left the boy's coat hanging on the windmill door, and there it stayed for the next twenty-six years until he retired. The mill was demolished four years later.

Some were more fortunate, finding new life after being converted into a dwelling, such as those at Cottingham and the extraordinary 'Exmill Cottage' at Finedon, which underwent a transformation in appearance, acquiring a crenellated tower, like other 'follies' of the manorial Dolben family, such as the former Volta Tower and Finedon Obelisk

Occasionally a group of enigmatic or symbolic motifs appear on the wall of a building. Some of these were connected with friendly societies that were founded in the eighteenth century as small local benevolent organisations which were later replaced by larger 'orders' or 'lodges' to help subscribing members in times of hardship, such as unemployment, sickness or old age. They often adopted imaginative names and were like freemasons in some of their ceremonies. One of these flourished in the shoemaking town of Rothwell, and a vestige of its one-time existence can be seen high up on a building showing, amongst other features, a face emitting rays above a group of figures and lettering, with the words 'Loyal Polar Star Lodge. Erected 1882'.

There is certainly a Masonic connection with a stone tablet in the wall of a former hostelry, The Castle Tavern situated in Lowick Lane at Aldwincle. Though connected symbolically, it is not in situ, having come from another building in nearby Titchmarsh after it was demolished in the 1950s. It depicts

The crumbling remains of the now sail-less windmill at Easton on the Hill.

the arms of Worshipful Company of Masons (three castles) and masonic tools in the form of rules and compasses, together with the date 1834 and the Latin inscription *'Credentes in Christum habent vitam aeternam'*, translated as 'believers in Christ have eternal life'.

On a house at Apethorpe, possibly belonging to a one-time academic, and next to the old school building is a decorative wall tablet on which is engraved a large shady tree, a bird in flight with its wings outstretched and a lengthy translation of a quotation from the poet Horace: 'If he hath not considered the vastness of the sky, or looked down upon the woods and earth and sea as through the eyes of an eagle, then he must fly'.

Two large stone tablets can be seen on either side of the gateway to Rectory Farm, Lower Benefield, with a 'then and now' scene engraved on them, one depicting a milkmaid in eighteenth-century dress and her twentieth-century counterpart on the other. Both are in contemporary dress, and each is holding

'Then and now' stone tablets depicting dairy farming on a gateway at Lower Benefield.

a jug and standing by a cow – giving a fine sense of historical continuity to what has been carried on at the farm throughout the ages.

In the courtyard of The Talbot at Oundle is a small stone tablet that reads 'I. S. 1775' and depicts three tuns, the arms of the Worshipful Company of Brewers. The initials stood for John Smith, who had a brewery nearby at the end of North Street from 1775 to 1962. One of four existing in the town in the nineteenth century, it was the first to open and the last to close. When the building was demolished, the tablet was moved to its present site. Two previous names of a former hostelry connected with the brewery, the Black Pots and later became the Half Moon, are both commemorated in the 'new' name of the adjoining side street and houses built on the site.

Other stone tablets occur in more obscure places and have even more unusual inscriptions. One such example can be found in a wall at Kingscliffe in Hall Yard, commemorating the donation of land (the adjoining wide area leading to the church) in 1897 by benefactor, Thomas J. Law to the village churchwardens. Kingscliffe also has two other interesting stone tablets of note, both to be seen on buildings along the Apethorpe Road (School Hill). The first can be glimpsed through the gateway of the former schoolmaster's house, above the wall of the entrance, and reads 'Books of Piety are lent to any Person of this or ye Neighbouring Towns', a reference to a library of nearly 200 books (now in the record office) which were provided for public betterment by the theologian William Law in the 1740s. Further along the road on the opposite side are the Cornforth Homes, built in 1891/2 by another benefactor, Catherine Cornforth, who, according to local tradition, walked to Birmingham in her youth to gain employment. There she accumulated wealth, some of which was later used to build almshouses for three men and three women. On the front wall, low down and almost unobtrusive, is a re-sited tablet from yet another village almshouse, that of benefactor John Thorpe, in Park Walk, which was built in 1668. Also in the same village at the Horsewater, between the rectory and the wall of the churchyard, is a slab partially covering a spring which was once one of the village water supplies. It has a curious pattern on the surface which has given rise to various interpretations as to what it depicts, variously a bull mace (or bulrush), a fossil or some kind of insect!

There was formerly a stone tablet above the well-head (now filled in and grassed over) at 'The Cross' at Cottingham, which was inscribed: 'Erected by the Copyholders, 1854, William Thorpe, John Spriggs, Bailiffs'. This was taken for safekeeping to a nearby garden, but has since vanished. The local bailiffs certainly took pride in their work for the community and recording it, for high up above the adjoining village of Middleton on the old village school are two more tablets; on one is the lettering 'Edw. Lynchley, Jno. Lambert, Sam Birdin, 1766' and on the other is 'Wm. Aldwincle, Wm.Hikon, Bailiffs'.

At Easton on the Hill is a stone tablet with an inscription commemorating a water supply provided independently by a local benefactor, Neville Day, in 1888. It can be found at the junction of the eponymous street name and West Street.

There are certainly other curiosities and objects of a bygone age to look out for around the county, too numerous to mention here. Some of these are not hard to track down, such as the highly visible, tall, crenellated grain silo in what is now the car park of the King's Head at Apethorpe or the tall pillar surmounted by a teapot at Deene, as well as the more common boot-scrapers outside certain dwellings or flood level gauges by a riverside. Others need a more careful, detailed search, such as the limekiln built into a hillside at Cottingham, but the results are rewarding, and the good thing is that, like archaeological artefacts, there are still others that have not yet been rediscovered!

On a final note, a word of caution sometimes needs to be given in places where there is a sign saying 'Manor House' or there is a stone tablet with an old date in the front wall. In the case of the 'manor house' the building may have been of some importance in the locality such as a manor *farm*. It would certainly be a building of some substance and stature but not a manor house as such. If there was not a resident lord of the manor (an open village), the chances are he would employ a steward, agent or other official to oversee village affairs or farm business, and be housed in such a building. (Sometimes jealousy could erupt if a neighbouring village did have a resident lord of the manor – a closed village – where a closer eye could be kept on the behaviour and actions of the inhabitants. Such a case occurred long ago with Dingley whereby the villagers, seeing the relative freedom enjoyed by nearby Stoke Albany and Wilbarston, referred to them as Sodom and Gomorrah!). Similarly, with a date stone, occasionally one must beware of taking one at face value. It may be from an original building that stood on the site and used in its reconstruction, brought from elsewhere, or if new-looking, carved in recent times. As with 'manor house' it may be purely accidental or unintentional, but occasionally it may just be that there have been delusions of grandeur on the part of the occupant, or blatant examples of one-upmanship!

HIGHS AND LOWS

Making a thorough search through certain documents can be very rewarding. All of them can reveal surprises, none more so perhaps than workhouse registers, school log books, quarter sessions papers, manorial court records, churchwardens' accounts, bishops' visitations, parish registers, vestry minutes, private account books and diaries – to name just a few – all of which reveal vivid aspects of a world we have lost. In addition, oral history also has its uses, as stories which have been passed down through the ages can often be the one and only record of a certain event, though one must beware of the 'Chinese Whispers' syndrome which can distort and colour what originally took place.

HOSTELRY TALES AND RECORDS

Three public houses in the county are recorded as having been forced to close on Sundays, for one reason or another, by a disapproving lord of the manor. In the mid 1800s, a member of the manorial family of Harrington, the Reverend Hugh Tollemache, who became rector for fifty-eight years, bought the largest of the village pubs (later known as the Tollemache Arms). Being an extremely pious man, with strong views on excess, he immediately installed his coachman as landlord and consequently enforced closure on Sundays for several years.

In 1890, a member of the manorial Tryon family at Bulwick was passing by the churchyard, when he encountered a boisterous crowd of villagers spilling out of the Queen's Head on the opposite side of the road. Outraged at such behaviour almost outside the church, and on the day of rest, he promptly had the hostelry closed – a situation that lasted for sixty-six years, until 1956.

In the following century – during the First World War – at Great Cransley, a group of navvies were engaged in work on the railway line from the nearby

The Tollemache Arms at Harrington – one of the three hostelries that were closed on Sundays.

furnaces to Loddington. One Sunday, the lord of the manor and his daughter were riding by the village pub, the Three Cranes, when they were confronted by a rowdy group of workers fighting in the road. He was so upset by such behaviour, especially in front of his daughter, that he ordered the closure of the hostelry on Sundays as a deterrent to avoid any future repetition, a situation that was to last for twenty years.

Other forms of unseemly behaviour have also been recorded, as at Gretton, where in 1840 the renewal of a licence for the Blue Bell Inn was refused because of the 'bad character of the landlady and the bad reputation of the house'. A petition, signed by a clergyman and a group of 'upstanding villagers' had been instrumental in leading to the refusal. What had been happening at that hostelry was not stated but it must have been extreme for there were an overwhelming twenty licences being held in the village at the time!

There is also plenty of humour in some accounts of hostelry life. An entry in the diary of the Oundle carpenter, John Clifton, for 21 October 1776, records:

Tom Nicholls and Polly Desborough were married today and a Jovial wedding it was, for the day was spent in mirth and Jollity and at night there was very elegant Supper in the Swan, for a great number of both Sexes who spent the Whole night afterwards in Dancing, and now and then a cheerful glass; and there was a rank of Old Matrons to look on the performance... and in their turn came in for a kiss or two, which was a motion that some of them had not gone thro' a great while... but they liked it!... Frisky, eh?

During the 1920s and 1930s, at the now demolished Cardigan Arms in the hamlet of Deenethorpe, the landlord, Alec Jones, offered a tongue-in-cheek free pass for use at the hostelry, subject to certain criteria being met. In addition he had a list of Ten Commandments pinned on the wall for customers to abide by. Among them were the following:

1st. When thirsty thou shalt come to my house and drink, but not to excess, that thou mayest live long in the land and enjoy thyself for ever... 3rd. Thou shalt not expect too large glasses, nor filled too full, for we must pay our rent... 6th. Thou shalt not destroy or break anything on my premises, else thou shall pay for double the value. Thou shalt not care to pay me in bad money, nor even say 'Chalk', 'Slate' or 'It'll be right'... 7th. Thou shalt call at my place daily. If unable to come we shall feel it an insult, unless Thou send a substitute or an apology... 8th. Thou shalt not abuse thy fellow bummers, nor cast base insinuations upon their characters by hinting that they cannot drink much.

In 1830, a drunken customer at an unnamed hostelry in Northampton announced to everyone around him that the vicar of Little Houghton had generously bequeathed one of his fields for the use of the poor in the parish, and that there was a great abundance of turnips there, more than enough for the villagers. Everyone cheered his announcement and drank his health. The next morning, men, women and children from outside the village could be seen helping themselves to as much of the crop as they could, before making their way home. Presently they were interrupted by the appearance of the angry vicar and his servant, both of whom were carrying whips. Everyone cheered when they saw him, but this soon turned to panic and confusion, as the vicar rode furiously towards them, making them scatter in all directions, leaving their farming implements and headwear behind them. However, it seems that they managed to get away with their free turnips!

Inebriation was usually dealt with in the adjacent stocks or lock up, but could also be punished in more extreme ways. In 1842, one such person, Annie

Gardner, was treated in a particularly severe manner when she was whipped outside the Chequers at Maidwell for standing on her head whilst being drunk and sent out of the village forever!

Though a one-time common name for a hostelry, the White Horse at Lowick (since renamed the Snooty Fox) is supposed to have originated in a village legend, which tells of a knight wounded in battle during the Crusades in the Holy Land, being brought back home by his faithful steed, whereupon it dropped down dead from exhaustion on the spot where the pub stands today, and which was consequently named in its honour.

On a much more serious note, however, was a blatant case of fraud and abuse of privilege which took place in the early years of the seventeenth century, one that affected a number of inns around the kingdom, including a maximum of nine in Northamptonshire (some of which no longer exist): the Greyhound at Middleton Cheney, the Red Lion at Creaton, the King's Head at Oundle, the Bull's Head at Kingscliffe, the Hynde at Gretton, the Talbot at Collyweston, the Talbot at Kelmarsh, the Plough at Daventry and the Reindeer at Towcester. It concerned a certain Sir Giles Mompasson who, between 1617 and 1620, was granted a patent by James I to license inns where appropriate. Prior to this, constables had the power to curb excessive drinking by imprisoning offending 'tipplers' and imposing a three year ban on unlicensed inns. Mompasson and his agents carried out their task of making lists of those places where they issued licences, from a reasonable 10s to an exorbitant £6, hardly affordable for most hostelries, who would have been more aggrieved if they had known that he was pocketing a great deal of the money for his own gain. So great were the number and nature of the complaints, that in 1621 he was impeached in parliament and his patent was revoked. Thereafter, the king solved the problem of tipplers and licences by ordering that any inn selling ale and beer had to obtain an alehouse licence at a standard set rate. The following is an extract from 1620, detailing five of the licences issued (at Middleton Cheney, Creaton, Oundle, Kingscliffe and Gretton):

CHURCH TALES AND RECORDS

Just as revealing are churchwardens' accounts, which, in addition to the usual disbursements for the purchase, maintenance and repairs to fabric and furnishings of a building, such as a new hour glass, or repainting the royal coat of arms and the Decalogue board (the Ten Commandments), give us a

Details from one of the fraudulent licensing records of Giles Mompasson, 1620.

glimpse of something once commonplace, but completely alien to us today. As well as summoning people to church for the service, bells would be rung on special occasions, such as high society weddings. The accounts for Hargrave include an entry for 1768: 'to Thomas Newton for ringing at the Gunpowder Plot, 2/6d' (This was a national custom of celebration instigated by parliament shortly after the plot after a petition by a county man, Edward Montagu of Boughton House, as a day of thanksgiving for the life of the king). Similarly, the accounts at Towcester for the years 1712 to 1740 record several other 'special ringings' such as those in July 1712 for 'the surrender of Dunkirk', May 1713 for 'the proclamation of Peace in London', and, surprisingly, decades after the event, June 1714, 1717 and 1718 'at King Charles's restauration [sic]' – each ringing being made at a cost of 5s. The same accounts include: May 1713, 'by ye consent of Townsmen for a Hogs Head of Ale which was given away upon ye Market Hill' (£2 15s); 25 December 1722, 'for Greens to Dress the Church' (1s); July 1736, to Mark Aburn for crying down a market on the Sabbath day (4d); and December 1740, for 'giving a Woman and two small Children to goe from the Town, having the Small Pox on them'.

Smallpox was indeed a problem, with frequent virulent outbreaks of three different types that could lead to death at the worst and disfigurement at best, and nearly everyone was a victim at some time in their lives. Early treatment for prevention – by inoculation – proved to be as contagious and fatal as the disease could be itself. In 1757, a surgeon, Edward Littlefield, set up a private clinic, or 'retreat' for recovery in Northampton at De La Pre, with fees varying between two guineas and four guineas, excluding sheets, sugar and any kind of drinks, for a standard two-week isolation period. Subsequent retreats were set up around the county at places like Badby, West Haddon, Helmdon, Nortoft Grounds, Thorpe Underwood and Stoke Doyle. It was not until 1796, however, that vaccination was introduced by Edward Jenner as a safer and more reliable form of prevention.

Other items appearing in churchwardens' accounts are frequent references to getting rid of churchyard pests, ranging from 'urchines' (hedgehogs) and 'aders' (snakes), to 'fullmart' (polecats – common at the time), that appear to have caused problems to the surface, like moles. In 1590, an order had been issued to all churchwardens in the realm, giving them the responsibility for the control of vermin within the boundaries of the churchyard. The accounts of Spratton for February 1784 record a sum of 4d being paid to Nathaniel Lansbery for an urchin, and Thomas Richardson for twelve 'old sparrows'. Hargrave's accounts note that in 1712, John Brown was paid 4d for a polecat, in 1714, 'a man of Brington' was paid 1s 6d for nine 'Hedghoggs' and in 1736, a man was paid 10s 'for an ader ketchen'. In Byfield's accounts for 1636, payment of 2s 4d was made for 'killing viij urchines'. Also in the same accounts of the latter village is an unrelated but intriguing reference the previous year recording the sum of 1s 3d paid to William Sewell for 'the bowling alley and twissell way'.

Churchyards also suffered from being used as a grazing area for animals, and worse still as middens and rubbish dumps. In a 1637 survey made for the Church of St Mary at Higham Ferrers, it was noted with disgust the appalling manner with which the outer area had been treated:

[it is] fearfully profaned with divers dunghills, and excrements... is so noisome as the people can scarce passe thorowe the churchyard by reason of the offensive sights and smells... noysome dung and filth, partly by scholars of the free scoole, and partly by adiacent inhabitants which ought to be inhibited, and partly by rubbish of the church, which ought to be removed.

Similarly, conditions inside the same church appear to have been no better e.g. 'the carpett of the Communion Table is like an old house carpet... The pulpit clothe and cushion are old and indecent'.

The Church of St John at Peterborough, however, seems to have had the situation under control, according to its accounts. For 1479, there is an entry: 'For clensyng and carrying of yearth and muck out of the churchyard about, iiijd.' and in 1504/5: 'Payd for carrying of the muckhill out of the church yarde, xvjd.'

As is well known, the Reformation, the Civil War and its aftermath took their toll on churches with bouts of general destruction and iconoclasm. Some churches seem to have hit back in different ways. In Woodford Halse's accounts there is an entry for 1641/2: 'to William Glenne for new glasing the churchwindowes when ye scandalous Picktures were pulled Downe by Acte of Parliament.' Even more remarkable, though not recorded, is what can be seen at the Church of St Mary at Brampton Ash. If one looks very carefully, it will be noticed that on one of the window panes (quarries) above the altar, is an inscription 'John Fanster, Plumber and Glazier from Bath, 1648'. One wonders if this was a Parliamentary soldier who had returned with a conscience, after his compatriots had been a little over-zealous in their activities there.

Another problem in churches was unruly dogs. Since owners took their dogs with them when they went to services, there could obviously be some kind of disruption such as barking and urinating – even running around the priest taking the service! Before the Reformation this would have been less so, since the rood screen, which separated the nave (a secular area used alternatively for social events) from the chancel and sanctuary where the altar stood, formed some form of barrier. When these were removed during Henry VIII's reign, it left the sacred area more vulnerable. In the Elizabethan era, the problem was resolved with the installation of altar rails (made compulsory by Archbishop Laude in 1634) and the employment of dog handlers with whips or collapsible tongs. Many parishes in Northamptonshire employed a dog whipper to handle the situation. Once again the accounts at Byfield provide some references, and one in 1637 records a payment of 9d made 'to Batts for whipping doggs'. At Woodford Halse, in 1641, the accounts refer to a payment of 8d 'to West for whipping Doggs out of ye churche'. By the end of the eighteenth century, however, references to such payments disappeared, as common sense began to prevail and dogs were forbidden to enter a church.

Even more interesting are occasional references in parish registers to another constant problem: parishioners falling asleep during the service! An entry for

Clipston in 1794 records 'Nathaniel Mott, weaver and gardener, appointed verger, to carry a white wand at service time to keep ye drowsy awake, to rap soundly ye sleepy heads, and also to keep decent order ye Sunday School children.' For this duty, he would receive 5s allowance from the church and 10s 6d allowance from the school.

Perhaps this was better than being observed by a minor late-medieval demon, called Tutivillus, whose role supposedly was to watch out for any idle chatter from worshippers, notably women, during the service or sermon, and make a note of who and what was said, for consideration on Judgment Day, when souls were destined for either heaven or hell. It is odd that any supernatural being on the side of evil was even allowed into a church! Yet his image was sometimes painted above the chancel in a Doom scene, just to remind the would-be gossiper who he was and to be on their best behaviour. In any case, it was simply yet another, more supernatural, form of social control.

Parishioners also had to watch out if they regularly spent their time in a pub, instead of being in church. Churchwardens were empowered to visit a hostelry to see if anyone was drinking during 'the prohibited hours' – punishable by being placed in the stocks for public humiliation within the community. More outrageous, however, was the comment made by one particular man at Walgrave in the 1800s. When asked why he rarely attended church, he replied: 'Sir I has to work sixty hours a week. I've got a wife and ten child'n to look after. And an acre of garden ground to tend. Sorry sir, but I ain't got time to be religious.'

It must have been a chaotic scene going to church in past times, having to tolerate the jostling, pushing, shoving, scrambling for a favourite seat, spitting, knitting, cracking jokes, hearing or making coarse remarks, to name just a few of the things that went on. Swearing, however, was yet another punishable offence. In 1695, William III passed a new Act, aimed at the suppression of profane swearing by 'any servant, any common soldier and common yeoman' by imposing a fine of 1s for each oath, and for anyone of a higher status 2s – the money to go to the parish poor. Refusal to pay would lead to the seizure of one's possessions (if any), or a period of at least one hour in the stocks. Inevitably, offences would be committed, especially if a sermon was particularly boring or rambling, as at Kingsthorpe in April 1698 when Sam Whitsey was placed in the stocks for swearing four times. In October of that year in the same parish, Peter Barrett was fined 10s for five oaths and five of 'profane cursing'. At All Saints' church in Northampton in July 1729, an 'un-named' gentleman was fined a massive total of £4 12s for 'forty awful oaths' and six 'swearings' for his volubility.

Early parish registers, with their records of births, deaths and marriages, show us the fragility of life as it was. Life was cyclical (unlike our modern one of progression), geared to survival and the seasons, with ever-threatening famine and disease. Life spans were short (with some particularly notable exceptions) – forty for a man and forty-five for a woman – and, until the later seventeenth century, teeth, lung and stomach problems, complications during births, and work-related and domestic accidents were all commonplace.

Entries in the registers of Nassington, for the years 1604-1645, leave a sobering impression:

[1614/15] Joane Burton was buried the 7 of Februarie, by moone light about two o clock in the morning, dying in childebed & not trimmed.

[1623] William Lee the parsons Sonne of Croxton... casualie drowned in the river over against the Mill howe, was buried here upon the third day of Aprill 1623.

[162¾] A crisum childe of John Bendons buried 12 March it departed presently after it was borne.

[1625] Ann Hamblin, wife to Adam, he knockt her on the hed on the 8 December & shee was buried here on ye 11 of December.

[1634] Buried. John Sharpe the sonne in law of William Holmes was drowned in a well. June 2

[1634] John Atkinson servant to Mr Lee was cast from his horse & slaine Iulie 16...

[1636] William foster servant to Tho: Ricroft was slaine wt a timber strike coming down the hill From Yarwell 27 Maij...

[1645] 19 Sep. Buried Robert the sonne of francis Whitewell, the nose eaten of with a ferret & killed the child.

In the registers of Islip, 1763, 'William Blofield was found in Titchmarsh meadow, perished by severe frost', and in 1771 'Henry Baker, farmer, died before the sentence of ex-communication was taken off – consequently was refused Christian burial'. From Blakesley's registers, 1601, 'Richard Tomason falling out of a tree as he was gathering ivie upon the Lordes day, tooke his death wound and was buried the xxij the month of December', and in 1683: 'Two persons went to London 'to be touched by the King's evil' (i.e. to be cured of scrofula). Not so fortunate perhaps was forty-five-year-old Joseph Pope, who is recorded at Clipston in 1803, as having been run over by a chaise on the corner of the road and died the same week; a year before he was unlucky to have a leg broken at the same spot. And, to compound the tragedy, his brother was also run over by a carriage the following year!

Sometimes a whole village could be up in arms about someone letting the community down, such as scandal-mongering or wife beating, which they would often deal with in their own way in the form of 'lowbelling', whereby local feelings would be made known outside the home of an offender, by making a continuous deafening noise or by burning an effigy of the offender/s. In other cases, a more formal approach could be made, as was the case at Creaton in 1766, when churchwardens and two overseers put up a public notice regarding an incestuous situation:

> The inhabitants of Creaton have reason to believe a Clandestine Marriage is intended by Thomas Barrows of Creaton, labourer, and Mary Barrett, his late Wife's Daughter… no Minister will marry them, knowing in what Connection they stand to each other.

Six months later, another notice was issued, signed by the same churchwardens and two new overseers, adding that the village intended to put 'the Law in full force against so unlawful a marriage'.

However, crimes of a moral and spiritual nature were officially dealt with by ecclesiastical courts, which were presided over by a bishop or archdeacon. In addition to 'trying' clerics who had stepped out of line in some way, they could discipline ordinary parishioners for religious offences and marital issues. One fairly common offence they dealt with was fornication. Penance for this 'crime' was done in the following manner. The two offenders had to stand in the church porch for three consecutive Sundays, wearing a white sheet or shift ('a shirt of penance'), with the face uncovered, and holding a white rod. Then on the third Sunday, at the second peal of the bells summoning the community to the service, they would be led by the parish clerk or churchwardens through the nave towards the pulpit, remaining there in front of the congregation until the end of the second lesson, when they had to make a confession of having sinned, and with whom they had committed their offence against God. They had to repent, promising never to do so again, and urging the congregation not to do as they had done. Such an occasion happened at Wadenhoe in July 1763, when John Weekley and his wife, Sarah, went through this procedure, having been found guilty of 'fornication before marriage'!

At Helpston in 1636, a more public exhibition of another kind occurred, so serious it led to a presentment to the bishop:

John Wright snr is presented by the churchwardens for that upon the 27 Nov. last, being the Lord's day, at the end of Divine Service, he rose up in his place, and openly in the audience of the people, did irreverently, malaptly, contumeliously and with great impudent face, exclaim against the minister for ending no sooner, although he was not above an houre in Sermon as might appear by the glass. He confessed, pleading the sermon was not over till almost one 'o'clock.

For this outburst he had to do penance before the minister and churchwardens and to pay a hefty fee of 3s 4d for the trouble he had caused.

Transgressions were dealt with in a different way by Nonconformists. The following notes are extracts from a minute book of Rothwell Independent Chapel for the nineteenth century, listing punishable offences committed by members in that area of the county:

Brother Crozier for spending a day in the Alehouse and going away without paying his reckoning.
Walter Horn of Islip for being drunk and found in the stocks.
Bro. Smith of Burton for having no conjugal affection.
Sister Cussens for keeping a sinful wake-feast.
John Cussens for threatening to bash his brother's brains out.
Bro. Mansfield for his passion in the church meeting.
Bro. Baggerly for assaulting and riding over a shepherd in the fields.

Bishops' visitations (made either by the bishop or a representative) were made on a regular basis to check that everything was in order at each church in the Diocese, that parishioners were behaving appropriately and that each clergyman was carrying out his duty according to the rules. Inevitably, there would be a lot of criticism during these visits and some fascinating remarks made about some of the parishioners. In the latter case, the vicar of St Peter's in Oundle complained in 1573/4 that 'the people are in a state of the most deplorable ignorance and profaneness, living in the constant profanation of the Lord's day, by Whitsun Ales, Morris dances, and other ungodly sports'. Later in 1613, it gets worse with one parishioner, William Wortley, being reported 'for allowing a *Wizard* to come into his house to tell fortunes' and one of his relatives, Henry Wortley, who maintained that 'women have no souls but their shoe *soles*'! (He later recanted this assertion). At Middleton Cheney in 1578, one parishioner said he would rather listen to a crow in a tree rather than to the minister preach in the pulpit! At Aston le Walls in 1570, the curate complained that 'during Divine service, John Spylman publicly accused him of "lying like a knave". At Harringworth in 1587, Thomas Hayward was reported for disobedience in the church, by being found "looking upon a Lattin [sic] primer, not understanding anie thing therein and for kepinge on his cappe in most part of prayer tyme".' (Here is an odd situation since holy books for many years had been printed in English). At Moulton, 1578, Joane Tymms was said to 'be a scold and soweth discord amongest her neighbours'.

In the majority of cases, however, it is the priests themselves and those responsible for the upkeep of the church that bear the burden, for a variety of reasons. At Canons Ashby in 1578 it was stated 'they lack a font and the curate is not in orders. He is reported to be a *morris dancer'*. The first of the four accusations here at Preston Capes in 1591, is a commonly reported offence among priests: 'the Minister weareth not a Surplice, nor baptizeth according to the Boke and he refuseth openlie to admit any to give thanks after childebirth, neither dothe he marie with the ring'. In 1570, the rector of Great Cransley was reported for illegally keeping banned Catholic items: 'manie copes, pixes and manie books and other monuments of Idolatry' in a chest in the rectory. And among many examples of church fabric being found in an unacceptable condition are those recorded the same year at Holcot 'the church windows are stopped with bordes and durte', at Orlingbury, 'the churche is like a duffcote, and manie windows are broken' and at Draughton, 'a windowe stopped up, half with daubing and the churche is very dark'.

In many other cases, it is the churchwardens who are reprimanded. At Greens Norton in June 1570, they are castigated for not adhering to the requirements of the state religion, two items of which should have been discarded in the first years of the Reformation: 'The rood lofte is not downe; the Communion table is not decent, and the holy water stocke (stoup) is still standing in the porche'. Similarly, at Helmdon, in May of the same year, 'they have no poore man's box and the roode lofte is standinge', and at Woodford Halse: 'the rood loft stands and at ether church dore a holy water stock, and the seate ordained for the curate to say service is undecent.'

There have been rare occasions when a whole village has been excommunicated, albeit temporarily. One such case was Brigstock in

January in 1299. A week previously, Hugh Wade, believed to have been a cleric, or representative of the Bishop of Lincoln, had lodged at a widow's house during a visit to the village. Thieves had secretly entered his chamber whilst he was asleep, stealing goods and money from his strongbox. The matter seems to have been resolved later, though how or when has not been recorded.

Before the Reformation it was customary for the wealthier members of the community to leave something for the church in their wills and bequests, such an act of 'goodwill' being seen as helping to ease their time in Purgatory after they died. These are often of interest not only for what was left, but because many chapels, images, altars and guilds that once existed within the church are mentioned, that would not have otherwise been known about, after the destructive ravages of the Reformation. Most churches we see today, for example, have perhaps a piscina as the only vestige of a former chapel, in the north and/or south aisle, or just a Lady Chapel as the only survivor. Some churches (even smaller ones) had an amazingly large number of these now lost features, such as Alderton, which had 'Our Lady in the Chancel, and altars to St Anne, St Catherine, St Margaret, St John, St Erasmus, St Nicholas, St Sunday, and St Sythe'; and at Bugbrooke: 'Assumption of Our Lady in the Chancel, Nativity of our Lady, Our Lady of Pity, Our Lady in the Window, Our Lady's Chapel, Our Lady in the Steeple, the Jesus Altar, St Catherine, St Cuthbert, St Nicholas, Trinity, Rood, etc'.

The wills and bequests leave money or some other possession for the upkeep of one or more of the above features, or for the church in general, most commonly for a candle/taper – a lyght' – (especially for the rood), a soft furnishing or cloth, or silverware. There is also frequent mention of 'torches' (thick candles for requiems/funerals) and, more intriguingly, 'sepulchres'.

Sepulchres, better known as Easter sepulchres, were used from the eve of Good Friday through to Easter Sunday, during which time a vigil was kept by members of the community on a rota system for which they were provided with 'coals' for warmth, and 'cakes and ale' for sustenance. Some sepulchres were built into the north wall (never the south) of the chancel next to the altar, as at Twywell, Grendon and Marston St Lawrence, and should not be confused with funerary arches/recesses which can be seen elsewhere in a church, though there are some rare cases where the recess has acted as both, as may be the case at Wakerley and Corby. In most churches, however, the sepulchre was a transportable wooden structure brought into the church

The fine Easter sepulchre in the church of St Nicholas at Twywell.

for the holy festival. Whatever type was used, an image of the cross would be placed on the surface, beside which a candle/taper would be constantly burning. It is this latter feature which is common in bequests, for example at Wadenhoe, John Goodrich in 1525 bequeathed 'to the light off the sepulchre, ij strykes of barley'. At Great Oakley in 1526, John Bull left a more substantial sum, probably for mending or making a new structure, as 'vjs. Viijd. in money or catell to the sepulchre'.

Another facet of medieval life was the privilege of sanctuary, whereby, since its establishment during the Saxon era and reaffirmed under Anglo-Norman Law, anyone who had committed a serious offence could take refuge in a church without harm or arrest for up to forty days, by which time he had to take an oath before a coroner to leave the country via a specified port 'without straying from the highway' en route. A typical example in the county was that which took place in 1377 at Rothwell, when William Thorewell took sanctuary at the Church of Holy Trinity, after having slain John Godale of Cranford at Rothwell. At the end of his sanctuary period, like many others, he declined to go on trial and after being given the port of Dover as his departure point, he proceeded as custom demanded, out of the town wearing sackcloth, bareheaded and barefooted, carrying a plain wooden cross, directly to his destination. However, the county witnessed several examples of sanctuary where things did not go to plan. One such incident took place in 1322 when John of Ditchford was arrested on suspicion of being a thief, but took refuge in the church at Wootton, where he confessed to felony. He later abjured and began to follow the set procedure, but quickly abandoned 'the king's highway', fleeing over the fields towards Collingtree, heading for a stretch of woodland. A hue and cry was raised against him and he was eventually caught by the villagers of Wootton and neighbouring communities, but in the process was beheaded. His head was taken to the castle in Northampton by order of the coroner – a heavy price to have paid for what was originally theft.

Burial rituals, like wedding ceremonies, have changed over the years according to custom, and even superstition, such as carrying rosemary in a funeral procession and then throwing it into a grave. One custom, however, virtually unknown today, that existed until the early eighteenth century, and which was connected with virgin saints such as Catherine and Agnes, was the carrying of funeral garlands, known as 'Maidens' Garlands', by a group of mourners, on the death of an unmarried girl. The garland (like a small version of the May garland) consisted of real or imitation flowers, together with a glove or piece of cloth belonging to the deceased. It was then hung over an empty church seat in memory of the girl. The framework of the vast majority of the garlands would have been removed after a while, leaving no trace of their existence, but some surviving (re-sited) examples were recorded in the middle years of the nineteenth century at two churches within the county's boundaries. At the Church of St Mary at Little Harrowden, the hoops and white rosettes (made of cloth) of four garlands were attached to one of the arches of the nave. At the Church of St Peter at Maxey, on a window sill at the south-east end of the nave, lay a hoop, the ribs of which were adorned with imitation flowers and other ornamentation, with two wooden bands crossing each other at right angles above it forming a kind of open crown.

Up until 1666, the usual form of burial was either naked or in a shroud for the majority of folk, or in a wooden coffin for the wealthier. That year, in order to stimulate the declining national wool trade, an Act was passed requiring shrouds to be made purely of wool, a custom not repealed until as late as 1814. A certificate of affidavit was issued within eight days of internment, as proof that such a burial had taken place. A typical example was recorded at Helmdon, June 1680:

> Tho. Shortland, son of Thomas, being Dead was put into a Pithole and Bury'd in the churchyard of the Town... and was well wrapt in a shirt of Woollen and was let down into his dormitory with that vestment about his corps to the great satisfaction of the Law...

A more fanciful description was recorded later in the same village, in 1682, when Frances Pickering was 'shrowded only in a winding sheet made of the Fleece of good Fat Mutton'.

A strange event is said to have occurred in 1745 at Easton Maudit, when the apparition of the newly-deceased Francis Tolson, was seen walking nightly to the pond in the vicarage garden. It seems that he had not been buried in the customary wool for one reason or another and so could not rest in peace. Following custom of the time, twelve neighbouring priests were brought in to lay him to rest by throwing thirteen candles into the pond, which seems to have put an end to the occurrence.

The most unusual form of burial, however, was one that was stipulated in the will of Langton Freeman of Whilton, who died in 1783. He had been lord of the manor in the village, but took holy orders and was instituted firstly at Hellidon in 1735 and Long Buckby three years later, returning to his home village on retirement and never marrying. He gave precise instructions that his body was to lie in a feather bed for four days 'until offensive' (this was not done!) and then to be wrapped in a strong double winding sheet, and taken to a summer house built into the south wall of his garden, the windows and doors to be painted dark blue, and then locked and bolted 'for ever'. It then had to be fenced off with iron or oak palings and evergreens planted around the structure. Strangely, however, there is no record of his death or burial in the parish registers, yet the procedure was definitely carried out, the building eventually becoming ruinous and covered in ivy, and the body found many years later, in a mummified condition and 'with no wrappers'.

Another strange will was that of a Lady Villiers of Sulby Hall, who had a local reputation for being autocratic towards staff and villagers. On one

A standard seventeenth-century 'burial in woollen' certificate for Northamptonshire.

occasion, whilst passing through Sibbertoft on the way to church, she became furious on seeing washing outside one of the cottages of the manor and promptly dismissed the family from her service. Her will, seven years later in

1897, insisted that two black horses were to pull her funeral cortege, and that they were to be shot afterwards.

Another unusual situation occurred inside the Church of the Holy Cross at Milton Malsor, where the Reverend Miller, the incumbent from 1799 to 1823, had his grave dug in the chancel of the church whilst he officiated there. Whilst watching the work taking place, he decided the grave was not long enough, and told the sexton, who promptly disagreed with him. He consequently got into the space and lay on the bottom, discovering that the sexton was right!

Sometimes being in a state of penury could pay great dividends later in life. In April 1743 at All Saints' church in Northampton, a 'beggar's funeral' took place. It was that of Anne Johnson who used to beg in the streets of the town. When she died, she was found to be in the possession of £400 – a huge amount at that time. According to the *Northampton Mercury* she was 'buried in a handsome manner at *night*' (such burials being reserved for the aristocracy or the unbaptised).

Let us now look briefly at some of the more humorous situations that have taken place. In the nineteenth century, a rector of the Church of St Botolph at Stoke Albany decided that the sermon he had just given had not been long enough, and subsequently turned the glass upside down and started all over again! At the same church in 1885, an elderly woman put up her umbrella during a service to protect her new Sunday bonnet from rain which was pouring through the roof. (The church still has some of the original medieval timbers today, and is also noteworthy in having a wooden notice board in the inner porch stating: 'Men are desired to scrape Their Shoes. And the Women to take off Their Pattens before they enter this Church'.) More recently, in 1968, during heavy incessant rain, the roof of the Church of St Helen at Great Oxendon collapsed during Harvest Thanksgiving. Undaunted, the rector continued the service with an umbrella. Another rector at Greatworth, in the nineteenth century, was notorious for handing out heavy sentences in his role as a JP. One day he fell off his horse attempting to jump a wide brook, and, managing to stand up waist high in mud and water, called out to a boy standing nearby to help pull him out. The boy looked pensive for a while and then said in local dialect: 'Waal you wunt be warnted 'til Sunday, so you may as well stop where y' be' and then left him to his own devices! The Reverend Arthur Tomblin, vicar of the Church of St Michael at Great Oakley from 1864 until 1900, had taken a strong dislike to the lord of the manor who lived elsewhere at Woodford, supposedly over an argument as to who was the more respected of the two

A rare notice in the porch of the Church of St Botolph at Stoke Albany.

men in the village. He began to build a huge mound next to the vicarage, tearing down parts of the latter in order to increase the height and girth of the mound. He also began to introduce weird comments and ramblings into his sermons, one particularly offensive occasion had him reciting some vitriolic verse he had written: 'Here lies Sir Richard de Capell Brooke, a faithless friend, and a ravenous rook, and if he's gone to a lower level, let's commiserate with the Devil!' Complaints were duly made to the bishop and he was suspended from further preaching, although he continued to officiate at weddings, baptisms and funerals

Also in the nineteenth century, after a Court Leet dinner in Kettering one local clergyman was found sitting on top of the toll bar at around 2am 'whistling away merrily to himself'. Another clergyman in the area, with two livings, found a man trespassing for game on his land and tried to forcefully eject him, which led to a protracted struggle. He appeared at the pulpit a few days later with two black eyes. This run in must have had some effect on his memory, for at a later Sunday service he promptly announced he had forgotten his sermon but added joyfully that he had a copy of the Marriage Act 'that will be of some use to many of you present'!

There is also a touch of humour in some parish registers, albeit unintentional. There are often Biblical names from the Old Testament that look antiquated and odd to modern eyes. Stranger still, is this entry for a baptism at Kingsthorpe in 1600, in which the priest seems to be either guessing – or writing down the real names: 'Alice Noname, daughter of Nicholas Nobody, was baptised the 26th March'.

Finally, in this diary entry for 1801, there is more humour in the following piece:

> Old Mrs Clark of Astwell was buried tonight. She had her Grave Stone set down many years ago, but could not manage the Task. Aged 90.

OTHER RECORDS

In addition to the laws of the realm, communities had by-laws (from the Old Norse 'by' for village), which we still have today, though in not so oppressive or petty a form as those of the past. These were reiterated at manorial courts which disappeared in the nineteenth century. The following list contains extracts from a set of rules issued at Kingsthorpe in the middle of the sixteenth century:

> No householder shall fetch or send fire in a wisp to another's house, upon a fine of twelvepence for every offence.
> No inhabitant shall wash clothes at the public wells before daylight.
> No person shall suffer any kite, buzzard, or carrion crow to breed, and the young to fly away upon pain of losing twelvepence.
> No man or woman of the township shall at any time lodge any sturdy beggar upon pain of a fine of 6s.8d.
> The choice of a king and queen for the May Games shall be made upon Easter day after evensong, and he and she that do refuse the election shall forfeit 6s. 8d, and the bailiff shall distress the same immediately.

The great houses of the county also kept records of expenses for estate and household, as well as for personal items. The following is an extract from a private account book of Elizabeth Wentworth, (niece of Sir Thomas Wentworth of Strafford, who was executed for treason in May 1641) who lived at Rockingham Castle. The entry dates from 1655 and lists some of her disbursements for the year, and give a charming, contemporary picture of her lifestyle and habits, style of dress, forms of entertainment and leisure, as well as the costs for each item, many being out of reach of most pockets:

lost at cards: 2/-, a token for my Valentine: 5/-, to ye lame Soldiers: 1--, to ye chair man for carrying to ye Morris dancers when ye King was proclaimed: 5/-, for an Almanack: 2d, seeing a play: 2/6d, to ye Maids for their Garland: 1/6d, for patches: 6d, for binding a Book: 2/6d, half a pinte of water for my Fasce: 4/-, for Spring Garden Beef: 1/-, lost at tables: 3/-, for a Ballet: 1d, seeing ye popet play: 6d, a vizard mask: 8/-. Besides ye sumes mentioned in this Booke, to be recd. these sumes, must be said to my use: To ye French woman: £14/15/-to ye taylor: £44, shoemaker £3/19/6d, to Gandon for lace: £10, to ye seamstress: 16/-, for 5 yds pinke taby: about £2/10/-, for silke stokens: £1/6/-, for a lased hankerchiefe: £14.

In the above list, 'patches' were small circular pieces of silk or velvet used on the cheeks for adornment; 'taby' was a striped cloth for dressmaking (giving its name to a cat with that pattern); and 'vizard' was a face mask worn for disguise at masked balls/masquerades.

Among the workhouse registers and medical certificate books for Harlestone are listed the following entries made by a physician between 1857 and 1862, which disclose some of the stresses of living at the time, and, to modern eyes, a somewhat unusual remedy for certain ailments!

> 11th, 13th, 15th, 19th, 20th and, 22nd March: Dinah Bird requires a pint of brandy.
> 1857: Elizabeth Wood, an able-bodied person, is ill of fever and requires ½ pint of brandy.
> 1862: Eliza Gibbons is labouring under mental derangement and is in a very weak state. She requires 3lb of mutton.

In those days when few could afford a physician and there was no health service, a wise woman with knowledge of plant lore and the world of nature and a neighbour acting as midwife were the best option for most people. In the towns, however, a variety of suspect cures and remedies were widely advertised in newspapers and on shop and chemist's posters. Judging by the contents of many of these, the brandy mentioned above may have been a safer option! A typical example is a 'wonder cure-all' or 'cordial of Rakasin' which was available from 'Mallett of Oundle' and was advertised in an 1830 edition of the *Stamford Mercury* which had a wide sales outlet in the north of the county. One wonders what it contained as it boasted:

it is well calculated to cure flatulence in the stomach and bowels, all nervous complaints, whether from taking mercury for excess, or owing to an abominable vice or other causes, it removes pains in the back and head, horrid thoughts, frightful dreams, dimness of sight, palpitations of the heart, dorsal consumption, trembling of the hands from hard drinking, and diseases arising from excess, and will invigorate and strengthen the constitution of weak, sickly and aged persons.

Advertising in this manner was very common with tradesmen in both the later eighteenth and nineteenth centuries, for all manner of things. Some advertisements were in a long rhyming form, often quite poetic, such as that in November 1768, in the *Northampton Mercury* for Joseph Young who had a chimney sweeping business at the Horsemarket in the town:

In sable dress, I use the Art, That's black, yet uncorrupt my Heart
No other Care disturbs my Head, Than that to earn and get my Bread.
When Lords and County Squires command, Myself and Imps are strait at hand;
Smoke condens'd from ev'ry Hole I rake, Ready pence for ev'ry Jot I take,
When out at Top my Head I peep, I wake the Maids with Chimney-sweep.
The Cook she brings a friendly Meal, The Butler waits with a Horn of Ale,
In ev'ry Place I'm welcome made, And brisk pursue my Sooty Trade.

And spare a thought for someone having trouble selling his property (something that might strike a chord with some modern-day folk). In this extract from a long advertisement in 1783, Robert Goodman of Nortoft Grounds in Guilsborough describes his 140 acres of good well-watered land, the various outbuildings for all kinds of crops and livestock, including 'a cow-house to boot, where a Milkmaid may go without fouling a Foot', in fact everything one might need at a country estate. He finishes with the following lines:

There's nothing that's wanting to make me rejoice, But only a Chapman to give a fair Price,
And if Part of the Money should chance to be wanted, If Security's good, a Time shall be granted
A Doctor, a Grazier, a Farmer, all three, If they can't be happy – it's wonder to me,
For further Particulars, Call at the Place, And I'll show it to you as plain as the Nose on your Face.

This slightly off-beat advertisement appeared in 1780, for the village of Old, where there was a vacancy for a schoolmaster: 'Wanted to learn Children to Read, Write and Common Arithmetic. If he has a wife that can teach knitting and Plain Needlework, that will be more acceptable. And if he can Shave, this will meet with more Encouragement'!

Finally, James Wheatley of Clipston, a 'jack-of-all-trades', did not advertise widely, and perhaps he did not need to, since there is a reference to him in the most unlikely place – in the parish register. Perhaps this secured him a regular 'plug' at Sunday service! It refers to him as 'an excellent blacksmith, whitesmith, cutler, farrier, phlebotomist, 'qui dentes extrihere solit' (who extracts teeth), himself so clever a mechanic'.

LIFE UNDER FOREST LAW

After William I had established his control of England in the years following the Conquest in 1066, one of the first things he did was to secure the best areas of land for his favourite pastime of hunting. To do this he sent out commissioners on 'perambulations' around the realm to seek out and establish the boundaries of each designated hunting area, each of which consequently came to be called a 'forest'. These areas may or may not have had large pockets of woodland, so 'forest' (as any good dictionary will show) did not mean an extensive tree-covered area, but was a legal term, denoting an area subject to a set of rules known as forest law. Some of these areas would be extended under later monarchs, so much so that about one fifth of the kingdom would come under forest law in the medieval period. Only a quarter of this area was wooded by the twelfth century.

Northamptonshire was deemed to be excellent hunting country, so much so that a vast area of the county was divided into three great forests: Rockingham, Salcey and Whittlewood. By far the largest, and the most popular with William's successors, was Rockingham Forest which at one time would stretch all the way from Stamford down to Northampton, with the rivers Nene and Welland forming the eastern and western boundaries respectively. Because of its sheer size, it was divided into three administrative areas or 'bailiwicks': Rockingham, Brigstock and Cliffe. To the south of Northampton lay the smaller, but no less important forests of Salcey and Whittlewood which were divided by the river Tove. Adjoining the three forests were Bromswold (Bruneswald) to the east (which subsequently gave its name to Newton Bromswold near Higham Ferrers, and Leyton Bromswold, now part of Cambridgeshire). In the west, on the other side of the Welland, was Leighfield Forest (now in Rutland).

Forest law stipulated that nobody except the king with his hunting party (or certain high-ranking officials given limited royal favour) could hunt certain animals, namely boar, red deer, fallow deer and (initially) roe deer, *all* of

An image of a medieval hunt scene in Rockingham Forest.

which were termed 'venison' (beasts). In addition, forest law extended to the protection of woodland (quiet areas needed by the venison) and stipulated that no one could fell a tree, or part of a tree, by any means or for any purpose, except with the king's permission. These prohibitive conditions were to continue for many years under successive monarchs.

This meant in effect that even those who owned the land, much of it granted by William to his followers after the Conquest, could *not* do as they pleased on their own estates – something that caused a lot of long-lingering anger and resentment. As a poor compromise, however, they had the right to pursue 'beasts of the chase or warren', such as hares, game birds, wild cats, martens, foxes and wolves. For this privilege they required a royal 'grant of warren' and the employment of a warrener to protect against trespass. In one respect this was nothing new, for a similar practice had been in existence under the Anglo-Saxon thegns, the only difference being that they could hunt or do whatever they liked on their own land, and used private gamekeepers (woodwards) to safeguard their interests.

In return for living under forest law, however, inhabitants were given more generous common rights than those living in non-forest settlements (these 'out-commoners' had fewer privileges). Firstly, for fuel or repair they were permitted to gather and take any timber that was 'untouched by edge'

– naturally fallen as the result of storm, age or decay. Of course, all this was done according to one's interpretation of 'naturally fallen' and when the need arose! For something more substantial – housebote and haybote (timber for construction) – the king would grant permission in return for a small payment and under the watchful eye of a designated forest official. This small payment could either be in the form of money, produce or labour, an example being recorded in 1251 when the villagers of Geddington and Barford carried out a series of tasks for the king's bailiff who farmed the royal manor. These consisted of three ploughings a year, three days' mowing, and one day's nut gathering in the autumn. In addition, at Christmas each villager had to give a hen and at Easter between ten and a dozen eggs.

They were also granted generous grazing rights. They could keep cattle and horses in the coppices and forest wastes, a process known as agistment. Additionally, sheep which were generally excluded in most forests, were usually permitted to graze in Rockingham Forest wastes. Although payment was expected for grazing rights, it was probably less than that paid in those areas outside the forest and more beasts allowed per payment, which was made to an 'agister' – a type of rent collector. However, they had to be branded with a mark of identification, specific to each owner. Among those used in the county included a cross, a horseshoe, an arrow, an 'O', or some other kind of basic shape, familiar to the illiterate majority. This was a necessary procedure when a 'drift' was made – an occasional round-up and check to ensure that the correct number of beasts were being grazed for the sum paid and to prevent trespassers from non-forest villages taking advantage. In the autumn there was the additional advantage of 'pannage' whereby they could let their pigs loose to feed on acorns and beechmast. In addition to these areas, there were extensive extraparochial areas of open land for communal grazing, known as 'shires', the largest being Rockinghamshire and Laxtonshire.

Balanced against these rights were certain restrictions to ensure the well-being of the deer. The Fence Month was from 9 June to 9 July, when pregnant female deer needed peace and quiet and solitude in the period leading to birth, so everyday activities which might involve passing through a wood, such as packhorses and carts requiring the transportation of goods or produce, were discouraged by the imposition of a special tax called 'cheminage'. A similar, though longer, restriction was during the winter period known as 'heyning' (c. 11 November to c. 23 April). This was a time when food was less readily available, and thus no grazing rights were allowed so that the deer could feed without hindrance on what was around.

Since protecting the deer was the overriding concern, additional rules were made under forest law. Certain animals – namely goats – that caused damage to trees and were believed to taint the grass with their odour (thereby putting deer off feeding and dogs off the scent during a royal hunt) were not permitted to graze. Geese were not allowed because their raucous sound might frighten the deer. Greyhounds were not allowed to be kept except by the king's hunting party, whilst other dogs had to be 'lawed' (expeditated) which entailed the removal of three claws from the front paws, to reduce the speed of the animal and to avoid potential injury to a deer. For this procedure, the owner had to pay an average of 6d – something of a burden for the hard-pressed villager.

Under the long reign (1216-1272) of Henry III, however, some form of progress and leniency was made. Firstly, a forest charter was set out twice (in 1217 and 1225) outlining the rights and laws as they should be, one noteworthy section stipulating that 'no man from henceforth shall lose neither life nor member for killing our deer'. This implies that some form of mutilation or death were punishments for breaking types of forest law. However, there are no records of this ever happening in the three forests of Northamptonshire – fines (according to personal circumstances) or a term of imprisonment being the norm.

Secondly, for a considerable sum of money, small deer parks could be granted to any major landowner who wished to hunt the 'forbidden' animals. The Crown would always be looking for extra revenue and this was one of the ways they could ensure this. Deer parks had to be laid out according to strict rules, for any violation or non-compliance would lead to the privilege being taken away and a very heavy fine being imposed. On being granted a deer park the owner would receive a number of deer to keep and rear, on condition that an internal ditch and some form of fencing – either hedge, wall or earth bank – was erected at his own expense and rigorously maintained. Many of the ditches can be seen around the county today, some quite wide, like holloways. Vestiges of (later) stone walling can still be seen today at Kingscliffe, and Harringworth (the latter at a considerable distance from the village alongside a track to Bulwick), whilst at Wakerley the foundations of walling lie under a large section of one of the public footpaths in the woods, and at Badby Wood the entire length of the pale can still be traced.

Deerleaps, or sauteries – a device that allowed deer to get in, but not get out – were strictly forbidden. The first deer park created in the north of the county was at Wakerley in 1228; in the south, that at Wicken was created somewhat earlier. There were also two areas created in the royal manor of Brigstock in the early thirteenth century (though possibly earlier), namely the Great and

Rockingham Castle. Offenders were held in a stronghold by the main entrance.

Little Parks, which lay either side of the road to Grafton Underwood. The following is a list of those others that once existed in Rockingham Forest:

Biggin (Oundle)	recorded 1327 (Abbots of Peterborough)
Blatherwycke	1270 (Henry Engaine)
Boughton	1473 (Richard Whitehill)
Collyweston	fifteenth century
Drayton (Old Park)	begun in 1328 (Simon de Drayton)
Easton on the Hill	1229 (Alan de Lindon)
Fotheringhay (2)	(1) Little Park, thirteenth century (2) Great Park, *c.*1230
Grafton Underwood	begun in 1343 (Simon Simeon)
Harringworth	1232-1234 (William de Cantelupe)
Kingscliffe	thirteenth century
Lyveden	1328 (Robert de Wyvill)
Rockingham	*c.*1256 (enlarged 1485)
Wadenhoe	1298 (Henry, Earl of Lincoln)
Weldon	1306 (Richard Basset)

That at Wadenhoe is of great interest. The village is believed to have been re-sited later below the spur of land from which it takes its name and where it lies today, isolated from the church up on the hill. One theory is that this happened when the deer park was created. If so, it would have been in the proximity of a great manor house which continued to be on the same site well into the medieval era and, therefore, not exactly attractive to the deer.

In later years, under Henry's son, Edward I, another concession for landowners came into being, with a similar set of rules and costs as those for deer parks. These were private, or 'purlieu' woods, where a private gamekeeper had to be employed (as in Saxon times) to patrol and control the area in question. Among the rules were: no hunting at night, on Sundays, during the Fence Month, more than three times a week, or for forty days before and after the king's hunting visit. In later years, to ensure further control, a royal forest official, a ranger, was employed to drive back any deer that may have strayed off crown land and to prevent them entering purlieu woods.

Northamptonshire was a very popular hunting ground for many kings who either stayed at Rockingham Castle or at royal hunting lodges (termed as 'palaces') at Geddington, Brigstock and Kingscliffe, the most frequent visitors being John, Henry III, Edward I, and Edward III. In the south of the county, there were royal hunting residences at Kingsthorpe, Silverstone and Wakefield, whilst Fosters (Foresters) Booth was also a popular hunting lodge for Whittlewood Forest (on the south side of the building which partially survives, there is a raised decorative hunting scene on plaster). Edward I was particularly partial to Geddington where he and his queen, Eleanor, had a suite of rooms and individual chapels. The two-storied building had various stained glass windows, one of which had an image of his father, Henry III. It fell into disuse after his death and by 1354 seems to have disappeared entirely, like Kingscliffe, which had gone by 1462 (its rubble being used for building purposes in the vicinity of the church).

Great Councils of national importance to discuss state business were also held in the area: William II at Rockingham Castle in 1089, Richard I at Pipewell Abbey in 1189 before embarking on a crusade, and John at Geddington.

A huge retinue would accompany the king on his hunting visits, a colourful sight if a somewhat daunting, burdensome experience for local villagers, going about their day-to-day life. Different kinds of dogs, each with a specific purpose (tracking by sight or scent, chasing, or for pulling down a deer) were kept for the purpose at local kennels. Deer went under a variety of names, according to their age and gender, unlike today where we just have the names hart, hind, stag, buck, doe and fawn. There were names like brocket, brache, soar, tegg, and intriguingly, for a female roe deer in its second year, gyrle – which may well be the origin of our word 'girl' for a young human female, which gradually

The effigy of a forest official at the Church of St Peter, Little Oakley.

displaced the long-standing usual word 'maiden'. If a deer was chased by the king it was an honour (though the animal would not think so!) and it would be called a hart royal.

FOREST OFFICIALS AND LOCAL PEOPLE

Let us now look briefly at the way forest law operated. The boundaries were known to everyone, inside and outside the forest. They were clear-cut and highly visible in most cases, and had been since the time they had been determined by William's commissioners. Known as marks, metes and bounds, they took the form of some kind of landmark (natural or man-made) – usually a ditch, a boulder, a certain tree, hedge, mound, stream, track, hollow, a gap between trees, a bridge, a mill, and even the distance between the edge of woodland and an adjacent building.

A hierarchy of officials was employed to make sure forest law was being adhered to and to ensure it was applied efficiently. At the top were two officials appointed by the king and trusted members of the higher-ranking nobility, the chief justice of forests, based in London, one with overall jurisdiction over all the royal forests north of the Trent, the other south of the Trent. Their main role was travel round the country in their zones and to preside over the main forest court (see below).

Below them and acting on a local level were the wardens, also known as stewards or chief foresters, who were high-ranking men entrusted with the custody of game and wood in a particular forest. That for Rockingham Forest being based in Rockingham, where he also held another position as warden or bailiff of the castle, looking after its day to day affairs and ensuring everything was in order if and when a king came to stay there whilst hunting. Until the mid thirteenth century, when the first Assize of Arms came into being, he was the only person officially allowed to carry a longbow, which was his symbol of office. Despite their high status, some of them were not beyond reproach, one example being 'Richard' who was accused by Lawrence Preston, lord of the manor of Gretton, of abusing his position by 'diverting' timber felled for repairs to the castle and 'converting Crown property for private purposes'. The warden denied all accusations, claiming he was only using his privilege to take 'husbote and haybote'. The king promised to investigate on his next visit, but ruled in favour of the warden. Another warden was heavily fined for his goodwill (or making extra money!) after he had allowed 'William of Gretton, son of Mary' out of the castle prison (where he was awaiting trial for 'offences against the greenery') for a nightly visit home, on payment of half a mark (about 32p) and a promise to be back at daybreak! The visits must have been quite short as a lengthy walk was involved between the two villages!

Answerable to the wardens were several appointed foresters, who were usually from the yeoman class or minor landowners and were elected for the job by their neighbours, whether they wanted the appointment or not. Theirs was the most hazardous role of all and they were widely hated, with some justification. They were completely unlike today's foresters, their role being a combination of gamekeeper and policeman, some of them patrolling on foot, others on horseback, whilst looking out for poachers and trespassers whom they had the power to arrest, if they were lucky enough or not outnumbered. Wearing a green tunic, their symbol of office was a horn, which they blew at the scene of a crime to alert neighbouring settlements. They also had a supervisory role, overseeing the gathering of dead wood, or collecting any payment of cheminage. Their work was unpaid but they had certain 'perks' in lieu of a wage, one of them being use of a lodge or farm, for which they had to pay rent. They could also go could go to any dwelling, at any time, and demand food or drink for themselves or their beasts, during the course of their work. Like other forest officials, failure to perform their duties properly made them liable to a fine, or court appearance at a later date.

However, apart from carrying out the law, they frequently incurred the wrath of the local population by going beyond their remit and carrying out illegal practices, one of which was to impound a villager's livestock, forcing the owner to pay a small fee for the retrieval of the animal/s. Another, extremely cruel practice, was to remove the ball of the foot of dogs in addition to the permitted three claws – and charge an exorbitant sum in return. Most unpopular of all was their practice of setting up 'scotale' booths, forcing villagers to drink the ale they had made. In 1279, the following complaint was made by irate villagers to the king about an annual occurrence:

> The foresters come with horses at harvest time and collect every kind of corn in sheaves within the bounds of the forest, and outside near the forest. Then they make their ale from what they have collected and those who do not come there to drink or do not give as money at the foresters' will, are sorely punished at their pleas for dead wood, although the king have no demesne, nor does anyone dare to brew when the foresters brew or sell ale, so long as the foresters have any kind of ale to sell.

Little wonder then, that some of them would occasionally meet with a sometimes fatal accident! Others were somewhat more fortunate, such as Hugh de Nevill of Kingscliffe, an overbearing individual who seemed to have some kind of hold over his fellow officials, making them turn a blind eye whilst he prevented local villagers from exercising their common rights. After they had made several complaints, Henry III ordered him to comply with the law – or suffer the consequences.

As well as the foresters, there were other officials who were in a better position – the verderers. These were members of the local gentry or knights, elected willingly (unlike the foresters) in the county court. They were not answerable to the warden, but had to answer to the king. Their role was one of combined magistrate and coroner at various inquests (see below), working closely with the foresters when a forest offence was committed. Their symbol of office was a short-handled axe. The job was usually for life, but they could buy their way out if they so wished, either with money or by royal favour.

There were also regarders, who like the verderers, were elected by the knights and gentry. They would make a general inspection of the forest

A thirteenth-century list of attachments with details of forest offenders.

every three years to assess and prevent any damage to the woodland and to look for any signs of encroachment, such as illegal assarting (clearing of woodland for pasture or other purpose), or perpresture (the erection of a building). They also checked that dogs had been lawed and that no-one was in possession of any weapons or traps. There were twelve in each of the county's three forests. When they presented their findings at the main court, like other officials, any error or omission would be punished with a fine.

FOREST COURT RECORDS

Hidden in archives and originally written in Latin, the records and documents of the various forest law inquisitions and trials make fascinating reading. As well giving us a colourful glimpse into what life was like at the time for ordinary people, they provide a wealth of useful information, rarely found elsewhere.

They show us how forest law operated, and the harsh penalties for misinformation (including the slightest mistake in recording a particular detail) or failure in one's duty. Unlike most documents, those concerned with state matters or in the recorded annals of history (more concerned with the monarchy, aristocracy and church), they give the names of ordinary people, as well as their occupations and the way they thought and acted; they provide references to leper colonies and the poor, outlaws, the corruption of officials and those of some standing (especially priests!), specific legal poaching and hunting terms, classes of animal by name, gender and age, county villages and places that no longer exist (Lyveden, Coton, Stodfold, Churchfield, Glendon, Barford, Siberton,Newbottle) and original names like Uppthorp (for Upper Benefield). Above all, they show us the medieval calendar where, instead of recording the month and year like the modern calendar, events are determined by the proximity of the religious festival at the time (for example, 'the morrow of St Philip and St James') and the year of the monarch's reign (such as 'the thirty-ninth year').

THE COURTS

Three types of 'court' were set up to deal with forest offences: an inquest (inquisition), a court of attachment and the main court or Eyre.

A blow on the horn from a forester would alert the neighbourhood that a crime had been committed, a form of 'raising the hue and cry' for assistance. At the subsequent inquest, held as soon as possible, representatives of the four nearest communities had to give evidence before the verderer/s of what they had heard or seen. Helping a forester at the scene of the crime, attendance at the inquest and giving proper evidence were all compulsory and failure to do so meant a whole village, or 'township', being fined 'in mercy' (up to six marks – about £4), and sometimes more. This was not unusual bearing in mind the intense dislike and unpopularity of foresters, and probably also laziness or apathy, as well as the fact that the offenders frequently came from those villages themselves! Several examples have been recorded, among them:

It is presented by the foresters and verderers and proved on Tuesday, the feast of the Gule of August in the twenty-ninth year (of Henry III), when Henry de Senlis and other foresters had seen evil doers in the forest with bows and arrows and raised the hue upon them, the township of Wadenhoe refused to come and follow the hue, therefore they are committed to prison, and all the township is in grievous mercy...'

And at an inquisition was made by the four following townships, Stoke, Carlton, Great Oakley and Corby, who said that the said evildoers were seen with bows and arrows and crossbows and greyhounds and that they escaped, but that they could not ascertain who they were. And because the townships did not come, therefore they are in mercy.

It is presented... on the day of the Nativity of the Blessed Mary in the thirty-fifth year, that Richard of Clare, earl of Gloucester, was at Rothwell. And after dinner he went into his wood of Micklewood to take a walk, and there he caused to be uncoupled two braches (a type of dog), which found a hart in the same wood. And they chased it as far as the field of Desborough above Rothwell; and it was taken there. And at the taking there were present, Robert de Mares, with three greyhounds, Robert Basset with three greyhounds, Robert de Longchamp and John Lovet, the verderer, who had dined with the said earl on that day. Thereto, as to the said earl let the matter be dealt with before the king; and as to the said Robert, Robert, Robert and John, to judgment with them; and because the whole township of Rothwell beset the said hart, when it was taken, thereto, to judgment with it.

A typical inquest, however, would be as follows:

Walter of Oakley saw a wounded deer dragging a stick at daybreak in a meadow... the verderers came and saw the mad hind... but it died the same night. And an inquisition was made at the meadow the following morning before the verderers and foresters, by four neighbouring townships, Great Oakley comes and being sworn, says it knows nothing, except that it died of sickness. Little Oakley comes and says the same. Newton comes and being sworn says the same... Corby comes and says the same... [1217]

Visual evidence would be produced either in the form of the offender/s (if caught), weapons, arrows, traps, sacks, or both. The articles would then be kept for later presentation at the main court. If a slain animal had been found, the evidence would obviously not survive, so the flesh was given to the one of the local leper colonies such as those at Thrapston or Coton (near Rockingham), or to the poor:

> The flesh was given to the poor [of Geddington]. And the skin was delivered to John Lovet, verderer, to have before the justices of the forest. [1246]

> And the flesh was given to the sick of Rockingham. And the arrow and the hart's head and skin were delivered to John Lovet... [1247/8]

The next procedure would be presentation of any offenders at a local court of attachment (sometimes known as a swanimote), which was held every six weeks in the presence of the verder/s, the main purpose being to ensure that the miscreant/s would appear by means of 'attachment' at the main court when it was in the area. There were various ways of doing this, primarily the payment of a pledge (something like modern bail) by the offender or by other people on his behalf. The sum would vary between half a mark – about 32p – and two marks. (This was not a coin of the realm but a monetary unit for accounting purposes). If this was not possible, the offender's chattels (goods) would be seized or he was 'bodily' attached, i.e. imprisoned to await his trial. Once this was done he was entered on the list of attachments and had to swear an oath that he would be of good behaviour towards the 'King's Game, Vert and Venison of the Forest', until the main court met, and he was subsequently set free until that time. Of course, he could die before then and that was the end of the matter, but a common outcome was non-appearance when the moment arrived, in which case he would be 'exacted', in other words be outlawed, and his guarantors (if any) would lose the money they had put up for his appearance, and be fined for this! For example:

> ...William of Houghton and Robert de Feugeres were present at the aforesaid evil deed. And William the spenser comes and is detained in prison. And Robert does not come, therefore let him be exacted and outlawed. And William of Houghton does not come and he was attached by Robert the son of Roger of Benefield, Henry the smith, Geoffrey Meagre, Robert Kidenoc, Henry Kyte, Jordan of Upthorp, William the son of the reeve, Hugh the son of Maud, Robert the son of Inge, Walter the son of Alan, Bennet the cobbler, and Robert Mayden, all of

Benefield; therefore all are in mercy. And let William of Houghton be exacted and outlawed. [1255 Eyre]

Sometimes, miscreants from one forest would make their way across the county to another, to commit an offence, despite having unlimited opportunities in their own area. Such was the case of Ralph of Brigstock in 1253, who was amongst other miscreants being attached at the time. The nature of his crime is not stated, but whatever the situation, he would lose his livestock as a form of attachment:

Thirteen pigs were found at Brigstock. They belonged to Ralph of Brigstock, who was suspected of an evil deed with nets in the forest of Whittlewood. And they were appraised by the four verderers at sixpence each...

The court also tried offenders for lesser offences against the vert or greenery, that is, theft of a small quantity of wood up to the value of 4d. Here the verderer could act in a judicial role and impose a fine. Any amount of wood higher in value would require attachment for the main court, the Eyre Court or Forest Eyre (which took its name from 'itinerary').

Travelling around its designated parts of the kingdom (north or south of the Trent) the Eyre was presided over by the chief justice of the forests and his retinue. It usually took place every seven years, meeting on an alternating basis at the castles of Northampton and Rockingham. These were grand long-lasting affairs, for example in the year 1285, it met at Northampton, starting in June for Rockingham Forest, then after a short break, for Salcey and Whittlewood until September. All officials and offenders had to attend with the accumulated evidence, records and woodland regards. The cost of their stay could be prohibitive. The following is a list of expenses for a stay at an inn in 1348 for the Rockingham Forest Eyre (the original spelling is retained, and explanatory brackets have been added):

Supper: Chickens 11d, Rost Muton 17d, Pidgeons 5d, Bread and Ale 3/6d, Taille [teal] 8d, Buskyetts [biscuits] and Carawayes 5d, Wynne and Suker [wine and sugar] 20/-
Breakfast: Chickens 6d, Boiled Meat 10d, A Pece of Beffe 8d, A Pece More of Befe 12d, Eggs and Butter 3d, A Conye [rabbit] 4d, Rost Befe 6d, A Dish of Pike 3d, Bread and Beare ¾d [beer], Wynne and Suker 6d.
Dinner: Boylled Meate ¾d, Vealle 5/4d, Lamb 2/6d, Befe 2/4d, Paist [pastry] 2/6d, Pyes 6/8d, Roste Mouton 3/-, Rappetes [second helpings] 2/-, Bakynge of Venyson 20/-, Peper 2/8d, Butter 6d, For Payns and Charges in the Dressyng ¾d, Wynne

JAMES R.

Trustie and welbeloved Wee greete You well, letting you to Witt that as Wee are credibly informed there are many evil disposed persons towards our Deere and Game of our Forest of Rockingham that doe keepe Greyhounds and other Doggs Bows Crossbows Buckstalls Deerhayes and such like engines *to take and destroy our Deer* within and near unto the borders of the said Forest, contrary to the auncyente Laws and privileges of the same—By reason whereof our Keepers and Officers of the said Forest doe find themselves greatly grieved for presente remedy; whereof and for the better quiet and preservation of the Deer and Game within the saide Forest and near unto the confines of the same, Wee reposing especial truste and confidence in Your diligent and prudent care in this behalfe doe earnestlie will and require You from tyme to tyme to cause diligente search and watche to bee made, throughout all the Baylywyck of Rockingham in our said Forest and the borders thereof for all such offenders and all such Greyhounds and other Doggs Bows Crossbows Buckstalls Deerhayes and such like engines and *all takers of Pheasants or Patridges* with their Netts and Engines as you shall find within the said Baylywick and neare thereunto likely *to do hurte unto our Deer and Game of our said Baylywick* You doe take into your Custodie and doe binde all such offenders to their good behaviour and all such as You shall find to doe hurte to *our Deer or Game within the said Baylywick* with Greyhounds or any kinde of Doggs or by usinge of any such Engines you shall commit them to Prison there to remain until our pleasure therein shall be fully known—And this shall be Your sufficiente warrante in that behalf given at our Court at Wanested this 21st of June 1610.

To our trusty and welbeloved *Sr. Edward Mountacute Sr. Christopher Hatton Sr. Edward Watson Sr. Thomas Brooke and Sr. Thomas Tresham Knight* and to every of them——

A seventeenth-century list of attachments with details of forest offenders.

and Suker 7/-, Bread and Beare 11/-.

And Horsemeate [food] for Mr Attornay and Commissioners horses 18/-

The evidence produced at the Eyre was astonishing in what it revealed. Some of the offences committed were extremely daring and contain acts of stupidity, even by officials. Here is an extract from one that was held in 1255 (the italics and brackets have been added):

It is presented and proved that on the Thursday next before the feast of John the Baptist in the thirty-eighth year, a beast was taken beneath the hedge of the castle of Rockingham by the men of the parson of Easton... And the foresters immediately after the taking of the said beast lay in ambush and kept watch through the whole night. On the following morning they found three men and three greyhounds; of whom they took one man (who was sent to prison but died before the Eyre)... Afterwards it was witnessed that (the deceased) and others, whose names are unknown, were with Robert Bacon, the parson of Easton... And because John Lovet contradicted his roll by saying that the said beast which was taken was a certain sheep... therefore to prison with him.

Note the role of a priest in the incident. Such an occurrence was not uncommon, and was sometimes violent, as in this record from the 1248 Eyre. (Note that the appellation 'sir' is not that of a knight, but was an honorary title commonly given to priests who had not matriculated). The form of killing used here – a modified form of a normal longbow arrow - was particularly nasty and lethal:

> Brigstock comes and being sworn says that Geoffrey of Sudborough, a chaplain, serving the church of St Peter at Aldwinkle with Sir Roger, the rector of the said church, stood on a certain oak in the wood of William de la Mouche and killed the said Stephen, a forester, with a certain barbed arrow...

The following incident in 1253/4, is remarkable for the sheer number of churchmen involved, whether directly or less so:

> ... the steward of the forest came away from the swanimote [court] of Cliffe, passing across the middle of the forest (bailiwick) of Cliffe through Morehay. Then suddenly and unexpectedly there arose before him and his men, with bows and arrows, Hugh le Moin, the parson of Thurning, Philip the tailor, Geoffrey of Wadenhoe, William the son of the parson of Thornhaugh [etc]... They say that Henry, the nephew of the dean of Oundle, Robert the parson of Polebrook, William of Burgh the parson of Barnack, the parson of Yaxley [etc]... are harbourers of the said evildoers... [1253/4]

It was also quite common for churchmen to claim some form of exemption from forest law such as claiming the right to be tried only by an ecclesiastical court, and to threaten anyone trying to impose it on them with excommunication by 'book, bell and candle'! This strategy did not carry weight however with Henry II who persuaded the pope that church privilege should not be extended to forest law. Offending clergy henceforth were, however, to be arrested by the bishop's representatives, though in practice forest officials continued to carry out this function.

Sometimes, however, there could be interesting developments such as that which took place in 1331, when Nicholas, abbot of Pipewell Abbey, together with two other monks were imprisoned supposedly for offences against vert and venison. Unlike secular landowners, abbeys were exempt from forest law on their own land where they could do as they pleased – cut down timber, build, and even stock deer, but if any of the brothers strayed off this land and carried out the same practices, they were bound by the same laws as anyone else. In this case, the abbot, during his imprisonment, accordingly managed to gain letters of release from Edward III ordering the warden of the castle to release them on bail until the next forest eyre. The warden ignored the order, until a further letter arrived accusing him of keeping them prisoner to satisfy his malice, and consequently, after a period of discomfort and misery, they were finally released. To add insult to injury, a group of men from the castle 'de-pastured' the abbey's grass with cattle at nearby Beanfield Lawn, took away three carts with nine horses sent by the abbey to take back hay, prevented the mowing of the grass and drove several of the abbey's animals (worth £100) to the castle where they were impounded and prevented from retrieval by the monks, 'according to law and custom'.

No one, it seems, was exempt from attack at the time. In another incident, the following occurred:

> ... evil doers were found with bows and arrows and three dogs in the wood of Brigstock Farming. And two out of about twelve of these evil doers took a certain Robert of Wick, the hunter of Sir Geoffrey of Langley, the justice of the forest,and bound him to an oak; and afterwards they permitted him to depart... [It is not recorded how long he was left tied to the tree!]

And scorn and a gesture against authority even extended to the king himself, as this event recorded in 1255 shows, when a group of eight men from outside the county made their way to the wood of Bulax near Lowick:

> (they) entered the forest of Rockingham on the aforesaid Wednesday, the feast of St Bartholomew, and during the preceeding two days and killed eight deer at least, and a doe, whose head the aforesaid Simon Tuluse cut off and put upon a stake. And the aforesaid Richard of Ewyas put a billet in its throat and made the mouth gape towards the sun in great contempt of the lord king and his foresters.

Normally, however, the offences were committed by local men, often with the connivance of a whole village. Even so, there were always 'spies' in the neighbourhood, and in some cases men did not take adequate precautions against being seen with their quarry; the expression 'to be caught red-handed' – literally with the blood of the slain animal on one's person – comes from this situation.

A typical incident occurred at Geddington in 1255, when among those attached were four foresters, as well as a page, Hugh Kydelomb, who must have been popular within the community, for the whole 'town' contributed money towards his attachment! It also transpired that he had taken some of the 'spoils' of the crime to the house of the vicar! The following extract gives other details of that particular incident:

Thomas the son of Fulk of Geddington came about the third hour into the park of Brigstock... and perceived a bowman with a bow and arrows and a page with him, who had taken a deer which lay in front of them. And they wished to shoot at the said Thomas and he fled, but he does not know who the men were. Afterwards Thomas on the same day towards night came to Richard of Horton and Robert the son of Robert of Geddington, to see in concealment if anyone brought the flesh towards the town of Geddington... they found Hugh Kydelomb of Geddington with four shoulders of venison, which he had retained, and one head of a buck with the whole neck, and one head of a doe with the whole neck. And they demanded of the same page whence he had the said venison; and he said that some men with bows gave it to him in the wood that day but who the men were he knew not. Afterwards they entered the town and Richard of Horton stood at his door, and saw William of Warmington, entering the town with a bow and arrows and a page who rode upon a sorrel horse with white feet and carried venison. The aforesaid boy when he perceived Richard, left his horse and fled. [but] the aforesaid William mounted his horse and crossed Geddington bridge with the venison and entered the lane towards the house of his brother...

The seven-year period for the court lasted until 1246. Thereafter it began to get more erratic, coming to Northamptonshire in 1255, 1272, 1285 (*nothing in the fourteenth century!*), 1490, 1556, and finally 1637. Obviously, there were valid reasons for this, such as two long-lasting (if intermittent) wars, the 'Hundred Years War' with France and the Wars of the Roses, both of which preoccupied successive kings of and nobles of England for lengthy periods, the social upheavals of the fourteenth century and also, and mainly, the gradual weakening and relaxation of forest law. This had begun in 1299, when Edward I, desperate as a warrior king for arms and manpower in his dealings with the Scots and Welsh, finally did something his predecessors had never done, despite petitions from landowners for more widespread hunting rights in the form of disafforestation – the freeing of land from forest law. That year, reluctantly (and which he later tried to renege on), he allowed a certain amount of disafforestation in return for much-needed help. This saw the subsequent slow shrinkage in the size of the three royal Northamptonshire forests over the next few centuries.

However, the Eyre of 1490 was something of event, its main concern being the alarming increase in the use of the lethal crossbow. It was not as accurate as the longbow (or 'Welsh bow' as it was frequently called), the use of which was still technically forbidden under forest law, but had been a vital part of the English army since the 1245 Assize of Arms, requiring all men with an income of over £2 – a considerable amount at the time – to be skilled in its use. The crossbow, however, was more cumbersome but had a devastating effect on any target, and it had become commonplace in royal forests, especially Rockingham. A series of restricting measures were brought in over the next few years.

Towards the end of the following century, the chief justice of the forest, concerned about the amount of hunting and the state of the forests, issued a 'request to friends' to keep an eye on the situation. Typical of what was happening at the time was an intriguing incident involving the heir of the manor of Great Oakley, Arthur Brooke, a man highly regarded by Elizabeth I, who had made him 'Master of the Queen's Hartshounds'. In 1591 he had been seen on several occasions by many local people illegally hunting with a group of friends. The situation had got so bad that it led to the Queen's attorney issuing a statement in April the following year, with the intention of getting him to appear before the Star Chamber:

> One Arthur Brooke, gentleman, Adrian Brooke, gent., Thomas Locke, Robert Dexter... [etc] being one long tyme here, have used to kill and steal deer in the Parkes round about them and to take their full pleasure and desire therein without the leave of the owner... and having grown so Insolent and Owtragious that they behoved to enter your Maties (Majesty's) forest accompanied with divers other disorderly persons led by the said Arthur Brooke, all armed with forest bills, Crossbowes, gonnes, dogges and other like weapons, did Chase, hunt and followe your Maties deare and carried awaye a Doe....[11 December]: The same party killed another deer and then hunted the whole herd so furiously that many afterwards died... [26 December]: the same party entered the forest again and trouped up and downe... and did kill a fawn and departed, taking the deere with them to the Howse of the said Arthur Brooke and there received and in verie riottous sorte eaten... where the said malefactors much triumphed in their said Enterprises and Encourage one another to bee readie to attempt the like again...

That same century also saw a major new development in the form of meritocracy, under the Tudor monarchy, whereby self-made men rose through the ranks, mainly in a legal and government capacity, and built large houses and estates reflecting their new-found status and wealth. This included the creation of ornamental deerparks – not for hunting, but as a landscape feature; these began to appear all round the county in places like Deene Park, Boughton House and Althorp House.

Some of the parks had an additional feature such as a 'conygear' or rabbit warren – a once-common name (with variations in spelling) in the landscape around the county. Today their former existence can be seen in the form of a pillow mound, an oval, circular or cigar-shaped feature something like a prehistoric burial mound in appearance. Unlike the hare, the rabbit was not native to this country and was introduced by the Normans (probably from their Sicilian territory) into our somewhat less benevolent climate. Like the hare, however, it was believed to be surface-living, and so the mounds were created for them to burrow down below until they could acclimatise – at least that seems to be the thinking behind their creation. The young of the coney was called a rabbit – this name eventually replacing that of the adult (and the young becoming known as a 'kit'). They were a good supply of food, and their skins could fetch high prices in the large towns around the country. One exceptional case is that of Thomas Tresham of Rushton Hall, who made a considerable amount of extra income from the sale of furs in London via carriers leaving from Rushton three times a week. The meat and skins would fetch between £3 and £10 (depending on what type of fur and colour – grey, black, or 'rich'). To house the warrener, he built the unique 'Triangular Lodge' (a Victorian name) originally called, successively, The Warrener's Triangular Lodge, Trinity House, and Three Square Lodge. It was built in this fashion, with everything in multiples of three, to reflect his secret adherence to the Catholic faith and the Holy Trinity.

A disturbing situation, tantamount to anarchy, had been occurring at Salcey Forest. In 1571, the local officials made a complaint about liberties being taken by the local population, something that would recur two centuries later (whatever measures were taken on this particular occasion):

> As there hath been of long time notorious destruction in underwoods of the said forest, by a great multitude of poor people of divers towns adjoining, called stickgatherers, so there hath been in this present year, such outrageous doings by them in braking [sic], slivering and plucking up by the roots the underwood there, that without short and shop [sic] reformation, the underwood will be utterly destroyed; and the number of them are so great and so unruly and unreasonable, it passeth our powers to reform them...

After James I came to the throne in 1603, he was determined, as a passionate hunter, to preserve the traditional but lapsed prerogative of a monarch's hunting rights, and accordingly in 1610 issued a complaint to the four largest landowners of Rockingham bailiwick (Sir Edward Montagu, Sir Edward Watson, Sir Thomas Brooke and Sir Christopher Hatton) about the local abuse of those areas still under forest law and commissioned them to investigate and arrest any such offenders. At the same time he issued a proclamation for publication in all the churches of the bailiwick and to be read out to members of each community. It set out 'nine ancient laws of the forest' to counter the abuse of purlieu hunting.

An interesting event occurred in the early years of his reign at Brigstock, where, in 1603, the newly-created Earl of Salisbury wanted to sell off some of his land in the former royal deerparks there. He began making clearances which would have deprived the villagers of their traditional common rights (and probably a supply of venison). A group of 'lewd women' was consequently sent to distract the workmen in the course of carrying out his orders, but the work seems to have been carried out without violence after the matter resolved amicably with alms being handed out as a form of appeasement!

His son, the unpopular Charles I, went one step further – and one step too far. Looking for ways to top up the royal coffers for the support of his extravagant lifestyle, he initially disafforested some areas of land to those who had petitioned him, but thereafter resorted to extreme measures, firstly bringing back the old forest courts at the villages of Little Weldon and Kingscliffe to 'try liberty takers'. At Little Weldon in 1635, forty-six offenders appeared, with fines being imposed of between £2 and £20, Among them a miller from Brigstock who had erected a windmill at Corby Woods and a son of Thomas Tresham, for maintaining a house built by his father at Brigstock Park 'contrary to Forest Law'. This was followed by the resurrection of the Eyre Court in 1637 and the restoration of the pre-1299 forest boundaries in the county, effectively bringing back all those places left out for centuries and leaving them open at the mercy of forest law. This led to a series of fines being imposed for failure to send representatives to the courts of attachment/ swanimotes. Major landowners also suffered by being ordered to pay heavy punitive fines that not even they could really afford, totalling several thousand pounds.

In 1638 he provided a hot topic of conversation and anger in local alehouses, when his newly-appointed Chief Justice in Eyre upset the townsfolk of Kettering and neighbouring villages by ordering Edward Sawyer, lord of the manor, to employ a constable and other officials to make a search of every house within a five-mile radius, looking for poaching equipment in the form of weapons, nets – even certain dogs – and to take into custody any suspects 'until further notice'.

Remnants of the original walls of the deer park at Harringworth.

These measures did not last, however, when he found that they just did not work. The pre-1299 boundaries were therefore scrapped and the area of royal forest shrank even further, when the landowners, instead of paying the heavy fines, were allowed to buy their land back and extend it even further!

The Civil War saw the further loosening of the laws, as the traditional role and power of the royalty was thrown into question, and took its inevitable toll as soldiers on both sides plundered woodland and game as a wartime necessity, fuelling a drive towards final severance from royal interference and control. This cause was furthered with Oliver Cromwell drawing up plans (in 1653) that were never implemented, for 'the management of the forests 'in a manner less offensive manner to the people'.

During the eighteenth century, land that had been disafforested began to thrive under the private landowners. Although much of it had been converted to ploughland or pasture (and eventually divided up as a result of 'Parliamentary Inclosure'), extensive tree planting, particularly of conifers, including many 'new' species from abroad, experimentation and the use of new techniques and ideas, helped revive and transform the landscape of the county. It also provided a better livelihood by encouraging an increase in the number of timber-related crafts such as tanning and charcoal burning.

For land remaining in Crown hands, however, the opposite was true, as everything was in a pitiful condition, with the land being abused and the woods neglected and plundered. In the south of the county a series of remarkable events took place in the Whittlewood area between 1727 and 1728.

The so-called 'Whittlewood and Salcey Timber Stealing Riots' involved eighty 'townships', and led to 147 people being arrested – a fraction of those who had actually participated. Though the real purpose of the thefts has never been satisfactorily explained, the official version was that 'they suddenly had the idea they had the right to go to the two forests, cut down and carry away what they pleased as "coronation poles" [to celebrate the accession of George II], though what that connection with that event has not been resolved'. In all, 239 trees were felled with a combined value of over £400. The forest authorities had watched powerlessly over several months, before they called in the militia, which finally led to a sense of order and arrests. The small number of prosecutions was mainly down to people unwilling to inform on others, partly through fear of retribution, partly to conceal their own part in the proceedings and to divert possible attention away from those 'timber sticks' they had taken. In at least one case, information was given by a person already prosecuted for one offence, and unwilling to face a second. A list was made of those bound over to the assizes for 'unlawfully cutting down and carrying away several trees out of the forests of Salcey and Whittlewood'. Those with the highest number of miscreants were: Collingtree with thirteen; Nether Heyford, nine; 'Shitlanger' [sic], seven; Towcester, Syresham, Stoke Bruerne, Hartwell and Milton, each with five; Eastcote/Astcote, Courteenhall and Paulerspury with four; Gayton, Greens Norton, Roade, 'Silveston', Ashton, Wappenham, 'Soulgrave', Slapton, Wicken, Grafton Regis, Woodend, Whitfield, Potterspury, 'Causegrave' and Passenham cum Deanshanger, all with three; Falcutt, Brackley, Weston/Weedon, Whittlebury, 'Heavenscote' and Perry End, Maidford, Abthorpe, Yardley Gobion, and Blakesley, all with two; and, finally, Farthingstone, Hulcott, Helmdon, Moreton Pinkney and 'Woodburcott', with one.

By the end of that century, hunting foxes had long overtaken that of deer, and poaching of rabbits was commonplace among ordinary people, now usually on jealously-guarded private estates, patrolled by gamekeepers. There were still occasional incidents of illegal deer hunting, however, as in the following case recorded in the *Stamford Mercury*, 11 July 1788:

> At the Assize for Northamptonshire, Nathan White, for feloniously coursing deer in Rockingham Forest, after a former conviction for a like offence against the statute, was sereally [sic] sentenced to be transported for seven years

In 1792 an official report concluded that Crown woods were no longer of any benefit to the king or the people. In 1817, an Act of Parliament was passed officially abolishing the Chief Justice in Eyre, and the remaining forests of the realm were placed under a special commission (and subsequently in the care of the fledgling Forestry Commission in 1923). Thirteen years later, in 1832, another act was passed officially enclosing and disafforesting Rockingham bailiwick. It was the end of a long, colourful era, one that had seen so much drama and intrigue, and one that nowadays has long since been forgotten.

NAMES,
PLACES AND CURIOS

HOSTELRIES

Hostelries have always been fertile ground for the research of social history, not just for the customs and tales with which they are associated but also for the range of fascinating names they went under, whether beershops, alehouses, inns or taverns, all of which are known generically today as pubs. Although a great many had flourished before 1830, an increasingly larger number sprang up after a new Act was passed that year to encourage free trade and to restore beer as the national beverage, after the ravages of the national 'gin epidemic' had taken its toll on the country's drinking habits. This new act enabled any householder (in the rate book), to sell beer without licence, for a one-off small fee of two guineas. Before this, many hostelries had common names depicting a visually striking and familiar object easily recognised by the illiterate majority, a royal connection or a heraldic device associated with a manorial family. They were now joined by a variety of newer, sometimes more fanciful names, the choice of the patron, whose main occupation (in the case of alehouses and beershops) was as a farmer, baker, butcher, blacksmith, shoemaker and so on.

At one time the county had – and still has in one or two exceptional cases – some of the more unusual hostelry names. Those that have long since disappeared include the Three Mill Bills at Nassington, a reference to the tool used for dressing millstones; the Bill and Hatchet at Southwick, tools used for hedging; the Sow and Pigs at Little Oakley, a name derived from 'My Sow's Pigg'd', a one-time popular card game played among farmers; the Black Pots at Oundle, a reference to the one-time commonly used leather drinking vessel; the Three Lasts, also at Oundle and a reference to the wooden models of a foot used by shoemaker to shape the footwear he was making; the Dun Cow at West Haddon, Glapthorn and Wellingborough, usually a reference to the

The old sign of the now-defunct Gate hostelry at Cotterstock.

mythical giant animal which was milked dry by a spiteful village witch (in different places in England, including Stanion in this county); Mother Redcap's at Northampton, a general term for an alewife who brewed and sold the drink; the Sword in Hand at Blatherwycke, a symbol depicted on the arms of the manorial O'Brien family in the eighteenth century; the Gate at Cotterstock, Cosgrove and Finedon, the sign often depicting a five-barred gate and the verse: 'This gate hangs well and hinders none, Refresh and pay, and travel on'. A more recent sign was the PLUTO at Corby, the initials standing for 'Pipeline Under The Ocean', a reference to the tubes made at the local steelworks, for the transit of fuel under the Channel for the Allies forces during the Second World War.

Survivors are the World's End at Ecton, a name for an isolated inn (sometimes just outside a village) and the Wooden Walls of Old England at Collingtree, a seventeenth-century reference to the sturdy ships of the navy, a bulwark of defence for the realm. The Chequered Skipper at Ashton, formerly the Three Horsehoes near Oundle, was renamed by the naturalist, Miriam Rothschild, in memory of her father, who captured one of these rare butterflies in a local field. The Lumbertubs at Moulton was named after Lumbertubs Lane, supposedly used by local shopkeepers as a rubbish tip for various containers. The Ten O Clock at Little Harrowden is believed to have its origins in the early days of the postal service, ten o'clock being the approximate time of arrival of the foot post in the village, where the pub acted as a stopping point.

Several pubs disappeared after the 1869 Wine and Beerhouse Act, which made licensing the norm, with stricter control under a magistrate, whilst others changed name or site according to fashion or under different owners – a trend continued today. These factors, combined with closures in recent years as a result of home sales and entertainment, the car, and the attraction of larger town pubs, have seen the county lose an estimated eight hundred hostelries over the years.

CHURCH DEDICATIONS

It is only very recently that serious thought and scholarship have been devoted to unravelling the reasons why churches were given their particular dedications. Some of the churches in the county do not bear their original names, having undergone a change for various different reasons. When churches first came into being, the original name would have been given by the patron, whether a secular lord of the manor or by an abbey, in which case it would be derived from the origin of that person or the dedicatory saint of the mother house of the monastic institution. If it was a lord of the manor, his choice of dedication would be that of his own favourite or patron saint (if he had come from Normandy, a likely choice would have been St Giles, or St Michael – the patron saint of that province) or it might be his own first name or member of the family. Another determining factor would be the location of the village: woodland, riverside, hill spur or in an isolated area, certain saints being associated with a particular feature of the landscape, for example St Botolph and St John the Baptist are associated with bridges, gates and boundaries (the latter saint also with healing).

As a church became established, in many cases a saint with a particular function would be chosen that could protect and favour a community, according to its particular needs. The vast number of churches dedicated to

St Mary – especially in Northamptonshire – reflect the growing popularity of her cult in the eleventh century and also tended to be sited along the main thoroughfares of the realm. Being a mother figure, and the holiest person next to her son, she would be the ideal person to intercede on behalf of a community in times of need. The all-powerful St Michael, the archangel (not necessarily associated with hilltop sites) was the ultimate protector and fighter against evil, the guardian between three worlds, who would also be present at Judgment Day to weigh up the soul's worthiness for entry into Paradise – obviously someone to answer to. St Helen and St Margaret were associated with the protection of flocks, the latter saint also with childbirth and midwives. St Leonard and St Giles were associated with hunting, St Nicholas with trade and St James (the Great) with travellers. All Saints (All Hallows) was a popular choice with its comprehensive umbrella of saints with different functions – a good 'catch-all' dedication – and also tended to occur in open field sites where a church served scattered hamlets and farmsteads. Dedications to St Peter and St Paul speak for themselves, as founders of the church.

Over time the needs of a community might change and so a dedication would be replaced with one more fitting to the current situation. A fair percentage changed as a result of the Reformation, others seemingly forgotten or brought back later as in cases where a particular village celebrated the feasts of *two* saints at different times, one according to the church/agricultural calendar, one for their own particular church saint – a situation not uncommon in Northamptonshire.

Wadenhoe went through a surprising number of rededications, beginning with St Michael (and All Angels), subsequently with St Giles (until after the Reformation), back to St Michael by 1890, then to St Giles again after restoration in 1901, and finally back to St Michael shortly after the Second World War. Reversals also occurred at Pilton, beginning with All Saints, then to St Mary and then back to All Saints again. At Spratton the church went from St Andrew to St Luke and back to St Andrew. Piddington underwent three changes: from St Mary to St Thomas Becket to St John the Baptist. Many of those churches with double dedications lost one of them, such as Easton Maudit and Weedon Bec, originally St Peter and St Paul but became just St Peter. Others had the reverse situation, the churches of St Peter at Chacombe and Hemington, becoming St Peter and St Paul. Weedon Lois changed from St Peter and St Mary to St Mary. In the case of Ravensthorpe, a slight alteration was made, possibly as a result of pronunciation, from St Denys to St Dionysius. A late change occurred at Corby where the Church

The isolated Church of St Michael at Wadenhoe.

of St Peter was rededicated to St John the Baptist in 1900, at the request of the incumbent who was also serving the churches with the same dedication at Deene and nearby Stanion. Apart from these, and a few other minor dedication changes elsewhere, the following thirty-one churches within the county at one time were later rededicated (Our Lady and St Mary, recorded in both forms, are interchangeable):

Adstone: St John to All Saints
Barton Seagrave: St John to St Botolph
Bugbrooke: Assumption of Our Lady to St Michael
Byfield: Holy Cross to St Helen
Church Stowe: St Peter & St Paul to St Michael
Denton: St Mary to St Margaret
Edgcote: Our Lady to St James
Farthinghoe: All Hallows to St Michael
Geddington: St Andrew to St Mary Magdalene
Greens Norton: St Lawrence to St Bartholomew
Guilsborough: St Wilfred to St Etheldreda
Harrington: St Botolph to St Peter & St Paul

Helmdon: St Nicholas to St Mary Magdalene
Kelmarsh: St David to St Denys
Kilsby: St Andrew to St Faith
Kislingbury: St Peter & St Paul to St Luke
Long Buckby: St Gregory to St Lawrence
Luddington in the Brook: St Andrew to St Margaret
Marston Trussell: St Peter to St Nicholas
Milton Malsor: St Helen to Holy Cross
Newbottle: St John the Baptist to St James
Rothwell: St Saviour to Holy Trinity
Sulgrave: All Saints to St James
Sutton: St Giles to St Michael
Sutton Bassett: St Mary to All Saints
Syresham: St Nicholas to St James the Great
Thenford: Assumption of Our Lady to St Mark
Tiffield: St John to St John the Baptist
Wansford: St Mary to Holy Trinity
Wellingborough: St Luke to All Hallows
Woodford: All Hallows to St Mary

PLACE, FIELD AND STREET NAMES

Place name dictionaries often have problems when it comes to certain difficult or ambiguous meanings. Such a case is Blatherwycke, given in virtually every source as 'where bladder-plants or bladderwort grows' (Old English: 'blaeddre'). This seems very dubious, bearing in mind that this aquatic carnivorous plant, though growing in England, does not seem to have ever been recorded in still water or on wet soil anywhere in the county. Blatherwycke is one of a string of settlements along the flowing water of the Willow Brook. Until the fifteenth century it was one of two parishes either side of the water, the other being some distance away on higher ground and where the earthworks of the former settlement can be seen today. Today, one of the largest man-made lakes in the country can be seen there and is now the home of several water fowl, but this was only created between 1845 and 1847 by Irish labourers brought over by the manorial O'Brien family during the Potato Famine. The origin of the name may well be connected with a more familiar sight, sloe or blackthorn, which in Old English has two names, 'slah' and 'blaec(th)orn', or even Old Norse 'blar', meaning

The colourful new village sign at Blatherwycke.

'dark' (in the Domesday Book it is recorded as 'Blarewiche'). What may have happened here is that the latter form was somehow transmuted as time wore on into 'blath'. Other cases where this has happened are where Old English 'berie' (burh – stronghold) has appeared later as 'by' – confusingly the Old Norse word for 'village' (as it is in Scandinavia today) – as in the case of the following three places in the county: the former hamlet of Kirby, Naseby and Thornby.

There are also questions to be asked about the prefix 'maid' for Maidwell and Maidford, places 'where maidens gathered' (Old English 'maegden'). This seems odd unless the reason for meeting at these places was to collect water (but then this happened everywhere and was not a remarkable occurrence) or they were there for some other unknown purpose. The Domesday Book in 1086 gives the prefixes 'merde' and 'mede' for the two villages respectively. But there are also other similar Old English words that may also have been transmuted: 'maene' (communal moot point) and 'maed' (meadow, mead), and even a Celtic word 'maen' (stone), all of which should not be discounted (the latter language gave its name to Crick in the county, and perhaps the rivers Nene, Ouse and Welland). We must also bear in mind that the scribes who wrote down the place names were in many cases from Normandy and recorded something as they heard it, though there are strange entries such as 'Patorp' for Apethorpe! Clerical errors also occurred later in the medieval period, a notable example being 'Priors Hall' for 'Priors Haw' (wood) near Corby, where a 'w' looked like a double 'l' and was duly copied as such. This can be matched with another, more correctly written, 'Priors Haw' not far away near Woodnewton.

Unlike place name studies, field name research is comparatively recent, and has lots of potential. We have/have had some fine examples in the county, many renamed or lost after the land was divided up and parcelled during the eighteenth- and nineteenth-century 'Parliamentary Inclosure'. Most names are/were straight-forward and common, reflecting orientation (north, south, etc), position (upper, lower, etc), size (great, etc), type of soil (Hell's Kitchen, Sweet Acre, etc.), association with a particular animal, crop or occupation, and past ownership/tenancy. There is, however, an intriguing group of names deceptive to modern eyes that look familiar but have a totally different meaning.

Easter Hill (Rushton) meant 'land by a sheepfold' (Old English 'eowestre' meaning ewe). Christmas Hill (Litchborough) was 'hill with a cross as a boundary marker'. Wormstalls (Corby) got its name from Middle English for cattle and hence 'a field with summer shelters for cattle' (not to be confused with Old English 'wyrm' for 'snake', as at Wormpath in Towcester). Lunch (Moulton) derived from 'lynch' – ridges on a hillslope. Ham (Passenham and Titchmarsh) was either 'enclosure' or land beside a river (Old English 'hamm'). Dead Shells (Welton), was where a dead peasant (churl) lay dead. The early medieval 'Dedequenemor' in the Whittlebury area, refers not to a queen, but was the general term for a woman in Old English ('cwene'). Cat's Brain (Little Houghton and Maidford) means rough clay with stones. Life (Holcot) means a hill, from Old English 'lyth'. Leisure (Earls Barton) gets its name from Old English 'laeswe', enclosed grassland. Ghostly Leys (Brigstock) comes from an old word for 'gorse'.

Other names have a supernatural or holy connection. Apart from 'Scratland' (mentioned elsewhere) there have been associations with goblins (Old English 'puc') with Puckwell Hill Field (Glapthorn), the village of Puxley and two 'puckpits' in isolated areas. And at Nether Heyford and five other sites there were 'thurspits' (giant's hollows). Sites with a prefix of 'grim' usually mean 'green' but Grimsland between Benefield and Oundle, could either be from medieval English, or Old English 'grima' for 'demon'. Areas of land prefixed with 'jack' such as Jack Arthur (Great Oakley) were pieces of land left untilled in the belief that it would divert the Devil's attention away from the rest of the farmland, thereby preventing any misfortune. Sacred sites gave their names to Harrow Hill (Brington), the village of Great Harrowden, those prefixed with Weedon (heathen shrine), and the villages of Hellidon (holy hill) and Radstone (rood stone).

Cut Throat Lane/Field/Spinney (Great Doddington, Aynho and elsewhere) was nothing to do with murders or a place with sinister connections but simply a transmutation of 'cut through lane' – a short cut! Little London (Yardley Gobion, Gretton, Passenham, Silverstone, Earls Barton, etc.) was a jocular name frequently given to a resting place on a cattle-droving route as a reflection of the periodic 'increase in population' in that part of a settlement. The former thriving market town of Oundle, with its weekly market and three annual fairs would have been extremely crowded, and it had over thirty hostelries at one stage to cater for the thirsts of visitors and locals. Of course, these places would have had no toilets and so some kind of unobtrusive place for relieving oneself was necessary. Jericho, conveniently sited next to but hidden from the market place, would have been the answer. There is a reference/clue to such a name and purpose in the diaries of the eighteenth-century Norfolk clergyman Parson Woodforde, who wrote in April 1780 about the men working outside his rectory who were 'busy in painting some boarding in my Wall Garden, which was put up to prevent people in the kitchen, seeing those who had occasion to go to Jericho'. (Interestingly, in Hebrew, the name for Jericho is 'riah' meaning 'fragrance'!) Skitterdine in Wellingborough would have had a similar function, being in the vicinity of the major St Luke's Fair. And there were the two self-explanatory prostitute hang-outs, under the name 'gropecontelane', which were recorded in the medieval period at Northampton and Peterborough.

Other sites have had their names deliberately changed, mainly in accordance with the heightened sensibilities and sense of propriety of the Victorian era, sometimes earlier. The village of Shutlanger (where shuttles/wooden bars were made) was originally 'Shitlanger' (Old English 'shitel'). Boothville in Northampton was 'Buttock's Booth' and in the same area, Cow Meadow, where the Ladies Bowling Club played their games, was renamed Beckets Park, to avoid any bovine connection! The exposed site at Hanging Houghton, called Windhouse was originally 'Windesarse'.

WRITTEN IN STONE

We might call most of this section 'written in stone' because so much symbolism and hidden purpose resides in carvings and engravings within and on secular and religious buildings. If you see three short parallel lines on the outer walls of a late sixteenth- or seventeenth-century house, this was a secret way of showing one's allegiance to Catholicism in an era when the only the

Church of England was tolerated. Pieces of church sculpture smashed during the Reformation, or removed in the nineteenth century when the building was undergoing restoration, were sometimes re-sited on farmhouses and other large structures. These were not necessarily re-sited for decoration or as a token of the past but, in fact, as a form of protection against lightning damage or other potential mishap – a kind of superstitious relic.

Many of the figures seen in churches had two purposes: one practical, the other more spiritual. Gargoyles, as is well known, were used for channelling water away from roofs, and dripstones to deflect water from the stonework, but the often 'grotesque' appearance on them was to divert any form of evil away from entering the building. They are among a group of carvings I usually term as 'apotropaic' – that is, protective. Many of these can be found around the county outside on friezes high up around the top of a tower, in a row along the roofs of aisles and individually or in pairs by windows and doorways – all vulnerable points in the fabric of a church which might facilitate easy entry for anything harmful. Similarly, inside they are sometimes high up on the ceiling, often out of view of the public gaze, blending in with the woodwork or hidden in those usually unlit areas. More often, however, they are visible in the nave facing windows, and especially in the most sacred area, the chancel.

They appear in a variety of forms around the county, either as tongue pokers, girners (face pullers), 'green men', exhibitionists (male phallic figures or female 'sheela-n-gigs') and in double-headed or tricephalos (three-face) form. The Norman Church of St Peter in Northampton has the widest range and greatest number of these and other more decorative figures as friezes around the external walls, but some village churches, like St Nicholas at Twywell, have just as dramatic a range. Female exhibitionists, though partially eroded with time can be seen at these two churches, as well one highly-visible figure with legs apart on the corner of the tower of St Peter's at Isham, overlooking the traffic on the busy main road between Kettering and Wellingborough. Inside the north aisle of St Andrew's at Cotterstock there is a phallic figure, which at one time was described as a man holding a dagger! Another figure, albeit somewhat mutilated, may have had the same appendage. Known as the Rothwell Imp, like its more demonic cousin at Lincoln, it is flouting itself just inside the entrance to the chancel.

Multiple faces can be seen at Aldwincle St Peter and elsewhere; it was believed that doubling or tripling the features would increase the power and effectiveness of the image. More common are the aforementioned tongue pokers and girners, with many county churches sporting at least one of these,

A 'tongue poker' embedded in the stonework of a former bakery at Little Oakley.

such as that at Gretton and Stanford. There is also a large tongue-poking figure from a long-lost religious institution built into the rear wall of a former bakery at Little Oakley.

The most interesting of all, however, are the so-called 'green men'. Apart from Yorkshire and Lincolnshire, the county has more of these than anywhere else in England – over two hundred – mainly in the northern parts where the more durable limestone exists. The combination of face and foliage is a striking one, but this has made the image the target of so much conjecture and misinterpretation, with opinions and assertions ranging from 'a figure to warn the congregation of the sins of the flesh', 'a vestige of pre-Christian worship retained to reassure and convert the community', 'a fertility symbol' and 'a representation of the Jack in the Green in the May festivities'. There is perhaps a little of each of these implicit in the real answer: protection (whether visible to human eyes or not) being the prime purpose as I have outlined above, not just for the church but for the community, against famine and (where visible) to guide the individual on the right path – to flourish in life and not deviate in any way. It appears also on fonts (for the life to come) at East Haddon, Wadenhoe, on the former font of Brackley St James, on many tombs/wall monuments and in crypts (such as that at Oundle) – to flourish in a life after death.

The image was not known as the Green Man until 1939 when it was applied by a member of the Folklore Society who was visiting churches in her area and saw a resemblance to the figure in folk festivals. Appearing not just

One of a group of the finest 'green men' images in Northamptonshire, at Finedon.

in stone but in wood and stained glass, the figure exhibits the whole range of human emotions, from joy, sorrow, anger, pensiveness, tranquillity, lust, anger, bestiality – and even a hangover! The face may be composed of foliage, peering out of foliage or, most commonly, with foliage issuing from the mouth. In fewer cases, foliage issues from the eyes and nose (as at Warmington) or from the body (as at Naseby). Cat-like images are also quite common, such as those on the chancel arch at Wakerley and the pillars inside Northampton St Peter's. A double Green Man on a roof boss keeps watch over the former fourteenth-century undercroft of Southwick Hall, originally to protect the family valuables. However, the finest examples in the county – and perhaps in England – are to be found on the pillars of the nave and chancel at St Mary's, Finedon, swathed in a profusion of foliage; in the wooden vaulted ceiling of the nave at Warmington, eight of nearly every type of foliate figure are visible.

After the Reformation, the original role of the figure became redundant, but it remained on the tombs of the wealthy and as a decorative figure on furniture, furnishings or mantelpieces inside their homes. At Rushton Hall, for example, it can be seen on wooden panelling, fireplaces, woodwork and on a leather wall covering. It was reawakened, like spring after winter, in the nineteenth century and beyond in churches in a decorative role as part of the Gothic Revival and also placed on the façades of public buildings, such as the

The May Queen image at the Church of St Mary, Geddington.

Carnegie Library at Kettering and Oundle School.

There is a set of unusual carvings at the Church of St Mary in Geddington, where three figures can be found, possibly associated with the village's former royal connections as a manor and hunting centre. One is what appears to be a female figure with a circlet of flowers round her head; it is tempting to interpret this as either a May Queen, or even Eleanor, wife of Edward I, both of whom frequently stayed in the village. Where Eleanor's funeral cortege later stopped en route to London led to the subsequent erection of three Eleanor Crosses, only one of which survives. Also in the vicinity are a jester and what is popularly known as King Ise. The church also has a rare stained glass image of Moses with horns (after coming down the mountain and talking with God) – the result of a mistranslation of the Hebrew *qeren* which has two meanings, 'ray of light' or 'horn'. When the Bible was translated into Vulgate Latin, it appeared as *facie cornuta* (horned face), instead of 'shining face' and artists thereafter showed Moses in this manner for centuries.

Pre-Christian relics were sometimes incorporated into the fabric of some churches, especially Roman altar stones. Above the Norman double tower arch at Tansor is a small opening with one such stone built into it. Another forms the base of a font at Hargrave, and at Castor, an important former Roman site no longer in the county, an altar stone from that settlement forms part of the Saxon font. There may be other examples around Northamptonshire yet to be recognised.

A depiction of 'horned Moses' on a stained glass window in the church at Geddington.

External church features are often overlooked, usually because of weathering to the fabric, unless they are carefully sought out and scrutinised. Amongst them are interesting carvings at Brampton Ash (a bat on the exterior north wall) and at Wadenhoe where there is a cat pouncing on a mouse high up on a buttress of the north wall of the tower. At Glapthorn there is a sow and her litter next to an external east window, and low down on the quoins of the south wall is a seventeenth-century religious inscription. Groups of cat-like figures can be found on the west and north exteriors of the Church of Barnwell St Andrew and on the south side of the church at Blatherwycke.

Even today, images are carved in imitation of the medieval ones, usually with a tinge of humour – and with spectacles! One image can be found on the exterior wall of the Church of St Botolph at Stoke Albany, depicting Canon Frank Scuffham, a former incumbent. Inside the Church of St Peter at Oundle (and at Lyddington, Rutland) is a similar image of the former Bishop of Peterborough, Bill Westwood.

Votive crosses can be found, usually on the walls of the chancel (as at Geddington) or of a doorway (as Wadenhoe). They are distinguishable by the pits at the end of each arm of small crosses, incised with a dagger, usually by someone about to embark on, or returning from, a pilgrimage – a sign of protection or thanksgiving for a safe journey. Larger crosses, often of the

Votive crosses on the north wall of the chancel of St Mary's at Geddington.

'globular' or floriated variety, are consecration crosses, made when a church (or sometimes its extension) was dedicated by the bishop. These were often anointed in oil or painted onto the stonework and so the majority would have not survived, but where they were engraved they are still visible, some fainter than others, and are consequently worth looking out for, and at Islip, Braybrooke, Barnwell St Andrew, Corby (2), Brampton Ash and Oundle examples can be found. More common, however, are scratch dials, formerly used by a priest for determining the time for Mass. A series of lines or pits radiate from a central point where there was rod (gnomon) – now just a rounded hollow, which in some cases is now filled in – to cast a shadow from the sun (if it was shining!). Many appear circular, but the upper portion was for decorative purposes. Several churches still have at least one of them, some of which have been re-sited (as inside the porch at Braybrooke). Other churches have many survivors, as at Grafton Regis, Aldwincle All Saints, Twywell and Wadenhoe, all of which have at least seven on buttresses and walls on the south side. Also look out for a series of hollows in exterior walls, usually a sign of where arrow sharpening took place, as at Fotheringhay and

A 'nine men's morris' scratching on the porch seating at the Church of St Andrew in Cotterstock.

at Lowick where villagers used a grooved stone for that purpose – now part of a bench in the porch – and had the right to cut arrow shafts from the yews in the churchyard.

One feature, however, has been misleadingly named 'leper windows'. These 'low side windows', always found on the south side of the chancel at most churches in the county, were *not* provided for such people, but are more likely to have been for those who had missed Mass for one reason or another. The windows would have enabled them to be present 'at the elevation of the Host', the start of which would have been signalled by the ringing of a small bell – the sound of which would be heard at these openings.

Holy water stoups placed inside the church near the entrance, for parishioners to make the sign of the cross, were a standard feature before the Reformation. There are some survivors, however, in whole or in part at Islip, Ecton, Harlestone, Cogenhoe, Twywell, Aldwincle St Peter, Fotheringhay and Irthlingborough. Piscinae for washing the Mass vessels are common enough on the south side of the chancel and in former side chapels, built into the wall.

A unique fifteenth-century wall painting at the Church of St Peter in Stanion.

Not so common are piscinae on pillars (as at Glapthorn) and double piscinae – one for the vessels, the other for the hands, as ordered by a thirteenth-century pope – which can be seen in churches at Polebrook, Tansor and Woodnewton. Sedilia, stone seating in the chancel usually in a set of three for the priest, deacon and sub-deacon, are also common, but four-seat sedilia are very rare, occurring only at Rothwell.

Inside church porches where there is stone seating, one will occasionally come across a set of nine engraved pits or a square formation of lines. These were 'game boards' for playing a shorter version of 'Nine Men's Morris', 'Shepherd's Mill' or 'merrils', an ancient game using pebbles or other markers and played between two people. The shorter version, 'Three Men's Morris' is the forerunner of 'noughts and crosses', and starts in the same way, but then progresses to another set of moves. It is this version that was played in church porches. They can be seen in at least four county churches: at Cotterstock (pits), Oundle (pits), Kings Cliffe (lines) and Walgrave.

Tucked away upstairs at the eastern end of the Church of St Peter at Oundle, where there is normally no public access, is the unique survival of a Tudor garderobe – or toilet – complete with oak door. Its original outlet is now blocked in but still visible on the wall outside. The church has two other unique features, usually inaccessible: a former schoolroom above the porch with some of its original fabric and a crypt beneath the south transept with a decorative vaulted roof.

A unique discovery was made at the Church of St Mary at Fotheringhay. In 1989, a 'secret room' was discovered beneath the north porch that was probably a former ossuary. Covering the floor were hundreds of fragments of broken painted glass, pottery sherds, clay marbles, pipes, coins and human bones. Some of these items are now on display in the nave of the church. A collage made from some of the pieces of the glass, depicting flowers, animals and other motifs, was subsequently built into the east window of the Upper Room over the porch.

As is well known, few wall paintings survived the ravages of the Reformation and Civil War, although there are some striking exceptions such as those at Mears Ashby, Slapton, Croughton and Burton Latimer, but in the south aisle at the Church of St Peter in Stanion there is one of the least known of all. Painted in red, yellow ochre and white, and dating from the fourteenth century, it is unique in that it does not depict a saint, foliage, Biblical scene or Doom picture. Instead it shows a Christ-like figure before which a stag and a unicorn are paying homage.

Finally, some clocks have unusual features. That at Whilton has only three minutes between each digit, perhaps signifying that time passes quicker there than elsewhere! Other clocks (Stoke Doyle, Wappenham, Great Oakley, Farthinghoe) have only one hand for marking the hour, a vestige from the time before the pendulum was developed in the early 1600s by Galileo; until then the technical precision needed to measure in minutes did not exist.

HEADSTONES

In the churchyard, headstones are a rich source of social history. A considerable number record or conceal a tragedy of some kind, usually death at a young age from an epidemic, consumption or in giving birth. A careful inspection of the dates, especially those in the early years of the nineteenth century, will reveal groups of brothers and sisters dying before they reached the age of twenty-one, as was the case with seven children at Rushton and Kingscliffe and a particularly tragic set of inscriptions

The poignant seventeenth-century headstone at Maidwell.

about four sisters, across the Welland at Great Easton. Sometimes there is a standard verse attached, as at Weldon, to the Pywell children in 1805/6: 'A consumption deep, laid us asleep, My brother dear and I, Weep not dear friends in vain, But hope its for our gain, That we so young should die.' (Another brother followed shortly afterwards.) At Sulgrave, a flat stone in the north aisle within the church, contains three marble lozenges, tragically recording three attempts by the vicar's wife, Sarah, to have a daughter named after her. Each one is inscribed 'Sarah, the Daughter of J. Loggin, Vicar and Sarah his wife' then the dates: 'Born Nov j3. 1729, Died Mar 9, 1729', 'Born Oc. 9, 1730, Died Mar j, 1730', 'Born Sept 13, 1731, Died the same day'. (These dates may seem strange, but under the old calendar (pre-1752) the New Year began on 25 March, not 1 January.) Finally there is the inscription on a headstone facing the street at Welton to a six-year-old boy found starved to death.

Until the turn of the twentieth century, puerperal fever, resulting from a uterine infection, was the most common cause of death among childbearing women, as can be seen by the large number of inscriptions on headstones and wall monuments recording the premature deaths of young women. Probably the most poignant inscription relating to death in childbirth can be found in the churchyard of St Mary at Maidwell:

> Here Lyeth the Body of Lucy, the Wife of Robert Tebbot, sometime gardener at this Hall who dyed in Child Bed the 3 Day of November, Ano Dmi 1689, Aged 27 yeares, 3 moneths. Unhappy that nothing but death would sorely turne to give thy infant breath, a stroke severe yet in it heaven prove kind, A Lucy took, A Lucy left behind.

Other headstone inscriptions refer to accidents whilst working on the construction of the railway, as can be seen at Great Oakley and nearby Little Oakley. One person who was lucky to survive, however, was a man from Geddington who fell off the viaduct and was only able to walk thereafter with an awkward gait, leading to him being nicknamed 'Bent-Axle' Talbot!

Two other headstone inscriptions refer to firearms accidents: one at Deene in 1752, 'John York, shot by accident, with gun and femur salt-wise' and at Blatherwycke that of twenty-five-year-old Martin Blaydes in 1844, 'killed near this spot by the accident of a gun'. Less obvious, however, as there is no reference on the headstone, is the story behind the early death of Thomas Milley at Laxton in 1687. He and his wife ran the village alehouse, and one evening a band of gypsies arrived for some refreshment. When it was time to pay, there was an altercation which resulted in the stabbing to death of Thomas by the wife of one of the men. (She was duly hanged.) Another murder victim was twenty-eight-year-old Louisa Johnson, whose cast-iron headstone records her death in 1893 with the words 'He brought down me in my journey cruelly, And shortened my days.'

Until the nineteenth century, a wall tablet inside the Church of All Saints in Northampton, recorded a tragic fire accident in the town one February morning in 1792 at the Shoulder of Mutton pub on Market Hill. It described how the owner 'was obliged to leave his affrighted little ones hovering around their distracted mother' and how he managed to reach the roof of an adjoining building after a strenuous effort, calling for help but to no avail. It goes on to say 'His wife, children, and two lodgers perished in a short time. Their remains were carefully collected and decently interred in this churchyard.'

When Fanny Blaydes, the wife of the vicar of Harringworth, was returning home one Sunday afternoon in 1884 from a visit to friends at the next village of Gretton, the horse suddenly panicked going down the hill. She jumped out of the carriage, and fell onto the grass verge but the impact made her lose consciousness from which never recovered. Her husband had a memorial placed by the roadside, where it can be seen today, when not covered with foliage.

Pets have often been given similar treatment accorded to humans when they pass away. There are burials with headstones all around the county of dogs, horses and cats. Two horses were buried outside but close to the churchyard of Bulwick in the nineteenth century, though their headstones were later removed and placed by the entrance to the rectory. Cats are often cherished more than people by some owners, one such man erecting a memorial in a Northampton garden in 1777:

> The turf beneath this arching shade, by Beauty's tears is hallow'd made,
> This dust was once alive as thou, Think – thou shalt be, what is this now?
> Could winning manners, loveliest form, with nature's genuine feelings warm?
> Could female softness, manly fire, could gratitude with these conspire?
> To save a mortal form from his doom, Remembrance might have spar'd this tomb,
> Ask'st thou who sleeps beneath this stone. One to the noisy world unknown,
> One who secure of dearer fame, Marks not the marble with her name,
> Nor think the tear alone design'd, To mourn the loss of human-kind,
> The gentle maid who weeps her end, Can in a Cat lament a friend.

Similarly, the renowned antiquary, William Stukeley, said of his cat Tit on its burial in the vicarage garden 'an uncommon creature and of all I ever knew the most sensible most loving and indeed with many other engaging qualitys'. His friend, John Montagu, at Boughton House, was a great animal lover and would have no aged horses or cattle killed, instead providing them with a paddock in which to end their days. He surrounded himself with dogs – many of them strays he had taken in and which lie buried somewhere in the vast grounds of the estate.

Another type of headstone inscription records the occupation of the deceased, particularly masons who tended to have the tools of their trade depicted, as can be seen at Oundle to Charles Braddock and Islip to John Coles, 1810. A more puzzling monument, however, is a plain undated chest tomb at Laxton, with the cryptic inscription 'Near this Place lieth buried the generation of Masons'. Blacksmiths often had a standard verse engraved, as at Weldon where the inscription to John White reads:

> My sledge and hammer lie inclined, My bellows too have lost their wind. My fires extinct, my forge decayed, And in the dust my vice is laid. My coals are spent, my iron gone, My last nail struck, my work is done.

The effigy of Juliana de Murdak, with erased inscription, at the Church of St Mary, Gayton.

A witty inscription, supposedly to a drunken cobbler and punning on the tools of his trade, can be found at All Saints' in Northampton:

> Close without the narrow stall, Lives one who was a friend to awl. He saved the soles from getting worse, but cursed his own without remorse. And though a drunken life he passed, he saves his sole by mending at last.

Other witty inscriptions can be found at Burton Latimer: 'Here lies, aged three score and ten, The aged remains of Mr Moorhen, Note well, for hen read cock, cock wouldn't rhyme'. And at Dallington, there is an inscription to Marie Hart, nee Green, which infers that only part of her has faded away, for she was Marie Green before marriage and will continue as such in death: 'July ye 30, 1647, Since when in part, Here lieth Marie Hart, hath fading lien, Who was before And will much more, Be Marie Green.'

However, other inscriptions and depictions can be threatening or even sinister. At Bozeat, there is a warning inscription to any would-be grave robber. An Act of Parliament had been passed in 1832 expanding the legal supply of corpses for medical research. Perhaps John Partridge (died 1840) and his wife Mary (1836) had this in mind when their headstone was engraved 'May all the afflictions of Job be the lot that disturbs the remains of those that repose below'.

At Weedon Lois, a badly eroded headstone depicts a woman holding a cup of poison to her husband. She was said to have been burned at the stake nearby, the last person to be burned for treason for this crime. Whilst it is true that killing a husband *was* treason in ancient law, the assertion is incorrect – the last person to be burned for this crime in the county was Mary Fawson, at

Northampton on 8 August 1735, and the last to be burned in England for the crime was in 1789.

Another poisoning is associated with the Church of St Mary at Gayton, inside which lie the effigies of Sir Philip de Gayton and his wife (or daughter of the same name) Lady Scholastica, side by side. A daughter, Juliana de Murdak, was accused of being a witch after murdering her husband, Thomas, for which she was consequently burnt at the stake in 1310. During restoration work at the church in 1830, an image of her daughter was discovered within the chancel wall, with her mother's name gouged out. It was re-sited and now lies next to Lady Scholastica in the same recess.

On a brighter note, a fifteenth-century floor brass (at present under a carpet) in the Church of St Peter and St Paul at Nether Heyford depicts Sir Walter Mauntell and his wife as a young couple. Although brasses did not depict the actual deceased, instead being chosen beforehand from a range of designs in a pattern book, this one is unusual in showing the couple holding hands – a rare break with convention and fashion. (A similar feature is on the early fifteenth-century alabaster altar tomb – with traces of the original colouring – of Sir Ralph Greene and his wife at Lowick). It is doubly unusual in having an error in the date, which instead of reading mccccclxxxvii (1487), shows a cumbersome 'mccccclxxxixii'.

ADVENTURES INTO THE UNKNOWN

Of all the areas of Northamptonshire, and possibly the whole of the Midlands, no other site has experienced such a variety of strange occurrences as that around Rushton in the north of the county. Rich in ironstone deposits, and in an area of geological faults, it is also, according to dowsers and ley line enthusiasts, the intense centre and focal point of a vast grid system which is spread over a wide area. Nearby, in the adjoining limestone belt, are several swallow holes, cavities into which flood water and streams enter on a seemingly endless and bottomless journey into oblivion. There are also pockets of dangerous radon in the vicinity, the colourless and odourless gas that can accumulate in poorly ventilated buildings and can have an effect on the respiratory system, even causing cancer.

It is believed that many ironstone deposits, especially those close to the surface, may stimulate the latent properties and increase the potency of associated magnetic fields. These magnetic fields could affect certain vulnerable and receptive brains in producing visual or audible (or a combination of both) strange or illusory phenomena, which have consequently led to the vast range of traditions, legends and sightings, that have occurred through the ages, down to the present day, like black cat sightings, the phantom black dog, moving stone work, a grey lady, and so on.

Several of these can easily be explained, such as the dun cow rib at Stanion, in reality a whalebone taken into the church in the sixteenth century. The ghostly fiddler of Rushton and the phantom drummers at Rushton and Brigstock have their origins in the popular pastiche, *The Ingoldbys Legends*, one of a group of nineteenth-century printed works that struck a chord nationally and gave rise to other tales that were adopted in various places around the realm. Even crop circles, known in the majority

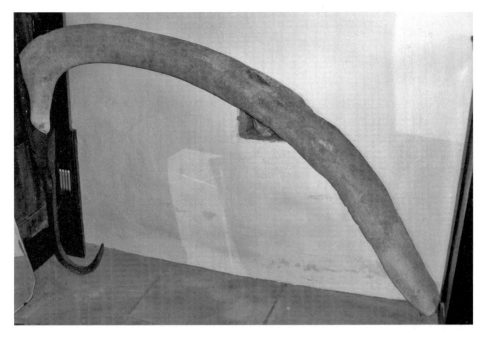

The 'Dun Cow Rib' in Stanion church, based on an incident which took place locally and elsewhere in the country. It is covered in seventeenth-century graffiti.

of cases to be made by human hand, have been seen when the air pressure and time of day have been favourable, by walkers off a track between Rushton and Pipewell, caused by one of the frequent small whirlwinds or eddies that occur in the area.

Others, however, are less explainable, like the ghostly monk that appears along the road between Corby and Kettering near the Rushton junction, causing motorists to brake or seen by them in the rear mirrors of their cars. In a spinney at the Newton turning off the same road, eerie whirring, dragging and clanking sounds were reported in 2001 by two metal detectorists from outside the area, unfamiliar with the local scene and its stories, working at night. Along the same road towards Kettering, strange aerial phenomena have been reported near and above isolated buildings in the vicinity. At Newton itself a few years ago, the daytime smiling apparition of a young girl was seen, with long hair, a white dress and hands clasped in prayer. She appeared to be floating through a wall at Newton, towards the site of a former graveyard where a row of children from the medieval period were found buried during excavation and building work.

The main geological faults in the area are those stretching from nearby Stanion, via Aldwincle to Twywell, and that in the vicinity of Kettering. There is also a syncline around Stoke Albany, where an ethereal mist has frequently been spotted, floating across the main road towards Brampton Ash and Dingley when conditions are perfectly clear elsewhere in the vicinity.

It may well be that some, if not all, of these factors affecting the local strata – confirmed by a geophysicist professor at Maastricht University – have been conducive to ionised gases from quartz being breathed in (like radon) and creating hallucinatory, respiratory and disorientating effects on anyone receptive or susceptible to such things. The earth's fault stretches across the North Sea from East Anglia to the continent, where similar phenomena have been experienced, a continuation of another weakness in the strata from Dorset to Yorkshire. This is comparable to ancient Delphi in Greece, at the Temple of Apollo, where a combination of two geological faults and earthquakes released trapped vapours from beneath the surface that gave the renowned oracle there its trance-like divinatory powers. These vapours emanated from a nearby spring and deposits of travestine, a light calcareous rock, which contains tiny bubbles of ancient methane and ethane, and from the same source ethylene was once widely used as an anaesthetic. It is perhaps, therefore, worth considering that which occurs around Rushton and not to just pass off many of the stories as pure imagination and gobbledegook!

Over the years, certain underground discoveries around the county have defied archaeological or historical interpretation. During the late nineteenth century, when workmen at Boughton were digging a pit in the lower part of a meadow for a water supply storage tank, they discovered, at a depth of about 2m, the antlers of a deer lying on a narrow stone pathway that 'appeared to be leading somewhere'. The surface was level and the stones were closely packed together, like a Romano-British tesserated pavement. Its purpose and significance, however, were never revealed.

At Welton in the middle of the nineteenth century, in what was once known as Stonepit Field, a 'rudely-formed sepulchre two feet below the surface' was discovered, containing two skeletons, beads of amber, glass and jet, a spear and some Roman coins. One contemporary unnamed witness, recalling his childhood days, wrote in the winter of 1907:

It is now on the side of a big bank so hidden by trees and undergrowth as to be difficult to access, and a small stream trickles past the front of it and it has flooded the interior. I fancy it was opened from the top only, and that the front

The skull under the floor of the Church of St Nicholas at Bulwick.

which consists of an open arch of cut stone which was subsequently laid bare by the action of the water causing the face of the clay bank to fall away from it. It has the appearance of a cave and as children we used to call it Robbers' Cave. On entering, you find yourself in a vault or chamber of some size, on the left side of which is a recess for a fireplace, with a chimney, and looking up it you can see daylight above. In the stone above the fireplace are two holes evidently made for the support of a shelf. On the right are a large recess, a cupboard or perhaps a sleeping place. At the back of the chamber there is another stone arch, blocked up by clay which has fallen from behind it, and streams flowing into the chamber. What lies behind that arch? No-one has had the curiosity to dig away the clay and explore.

Under the floor at the rear of the nave of the Church of St Nicholas at Bulwick is a skull embedded in a stone base, the sockets of its eyes staring upwards. No satisfactory explanation has ever been given, though there are theories that it was put there by a former incumbent as a joke. It is more likely to be an apotropaic device – a form of protection against evil influences that might try to enter the sacred precincts – similar to prehistoric foundation sacrifices, whose role was to guard and protect a site or dwelling, though these were, as the words suggest, a slaughtered volunteer or captive!

On the walls of the Winter Parlour at Canons Ashby House are a set of wooden panels that appear to have been tarred over at some stage, possibly with a black oily paint, and which have since been cleaned up and re-sited. There are seventeen of them, dating from the 1590s – the survivors of a somewhat larger number that have since vanished. They are of a 'carpet pattern' (or lozenge) type and depict a variety of symbolic images which beg interpretation. A few years ago, I was invited to try to unravel some of their secrets – a daunting task! Most of them, however, appear to signify a form of virtue or strength, others perhaps some kind of weakness – perhaps they are a moral code for regulating one's life, as can be seen elsewhere in the building in various Latin inscriptions.

I give some of my interpretations here: a set of scales (justice), five arrows, one of which is centrally balanced (harmony), a column surmounted by a lion (strength), a crowned figure on a platter (possibly authority), a figure with a slipped crown on a platter (possibly dishonour, or 'blindness'), a quadrant (temperance, or moderation), a boar's head on a cushion (courage), a hand holding a quill (intellect). Others include an upward-pointing dagger above a woolly crescent, or Masonic clouds, a scallop shell and a branch (possibly piety), and a lion rampant holding a harp. Ancestors of the Dryden family who inherited the house in the sixteenth century came from Scotland, in particular the south of the country and Border regions, and there appears to be a Scottish connection with the boar's head image (with no neck) for English boars' heads tend to include the neck. There is also a definite Masonic connection with some of the images, and the fireplace in the same room depicts a set square and compass, as does another fireplace in an upstairs room, which has embossed compasses on the stonework. Some might even argue that the lozenge/carpet pattern on the panels is a distorted octagon, eight being the perfect number and the basis of sacred geometry – but that is another story! Finally, the Winter Parlour also has a set of smaller panels each with a central scroll showing a different coat of arms, perhaps family connections of some kind.

When a large building was being demolished at Weston by Welland in the 1970s, there was an amazing discovery. Despite its age (late sixteenth/early seventeenth century) the house, which faced the church, was in such a state that some form of drastic action was necessary, and demolition was considered the best option. Whilst work was taking place on the inner walls, pieces of fragile painted plaster were uncovered depicting various fading images in colour. On one of these was the outline of what appears to have been a palace. More intriguing, however, was another large fragment

*One of the mystery wooden panels in the
Winter Parlour at Canons Ashby House.*

showing a female figure in a long dress, seeming to have been taken by
surprise, her head tilting backwards and a crown falling from her red hair.
To her right, a male figure in Tudor dress is confronting her. It leaves little to
the imagination that this was Elizabeth I. Why was it painted? Is there some
form of message or symbolism? My guess is that the occupant of the house
at that time was a recusant, at a time when it was illegal and punishable to
be a Catholic. The scene may be a form of defiance against the Protestant
monarch and her realm.

There is, however, an even more blatant form of defiance against the state.
In the sixteenth century, Edward Griffin, a staunch Catholic, lived at Dingley
Hall. Engraved on the porch was the inscription: 'Anno 1558. In the Rayne of
Felepe and Mary' – a scandalous insinuation that Philip of Spain – never made
king of England – was joint monarch with his wife. England and Spain were
not exactly on good terms at the time, and Catholicism was to be replaced
once again by Protestantism that same year, when Elizabeth I ascended the
throne, after Mary's death on 7 November. Intriguingly, since there is no
record of the month the work was carried out on the Hall, one wonders
whether the inscription was made before or after Mary's death. Whatever
the case, another inscription in the vicinity was definitely incriminating and a
treasonable offence. It read 'God Save the King 1560'. Elizabeth, of course, was

Dingley Hall as it looks today, and the home of recusant Edward Griffin in the sixteenth century.

not married at the time of her accession and never would be. Griffin, therefore, was taking a great gamble (especially if any royal or church officials were in the area), by flaunting his allegiance to an enemy, Philip of Spain, who was still alive and who would be responsible for organising the Armada against England six years later.

In October 1979, a traffic warden with an interest in history borrowed a metal detector from the RAF and was operating in the cellar of Rushton Hall, looking for the legendary secret tunnel that supposedly led underground to the Triangular Lodge, some distance away in the Hall grounds. He gradually uncovered a large cavity at the base of a wall. It proved to be some sort of entrance but not that of a tunnel. About 20ft in length, it had been covered up by a large wine barrel. He thought he had found a well but it subsequently turned out to be a priest's hole, a feature of the great houses of those who illegally held to the Catholic faith during Elizabeth's long reign and where Jesuit priests were concealed at times of danger. Items connected with the Mass were found on the floor including a communion bell, a key, broken wine flasks and some oyster shells. Outside the cellar on an upstairs floor there is a small room (not open to the public today), that acted as an oratory. One of the walls

The secret oratory of Thomas Tresham at Rushton Hall.

has a hollow sound and is believed to have concealed a form of access to the cellar below. On the wall facing the entrance there is a painted frieze with the date 1577 depicting the Crucifixion. The two thieves are bound, not nailed. At the foot of the cross are Mary Magdalene (her head uncovered and long hair flowing over her shoulders) and the Virgin Mary (swooning into the arms of other women). A mounted centurion surveys the scene, whilst soldiers cast lots on the ground below for Christ's seamless garment. One of the soldiers is bewailing the loss of a foot. In the background is a banner bearing the Roman slogan 'SPQR'. Interestingly, the soldiers are wearing a mixture of Roman and Tudor armour! In 1832, workmen making repairs in the great hall removed a lintel over one of the older doorways and found a breviary. They later took out another long stone, behind which were twenty Catholic books, in excellent condition, and several bundles of historical notes (some by Tresham himself) building accounts and family correspondence.

Tresham did not stop there. As well as paying vast sums of money for buildings that either reflected his religious faith – the Triangular Lodge (representing the Trinity) and Lyveden New Bield (representing the Passion) or the now-vanished Hawkfield Lodge, and the elaborate Market House (representing the Cross) in Rothwell – he held illegal secret masses at the Little Park in Brigstock. But he went too far on a later occasion in 1605, when, after years of adversity, he took advantage of being made 'Commissioner of

*The Triangular Lodge at Rushton,
supposedly built by Thomas Tresham for
the warrener on the estate, but in reality a
secretly coded design reflecting his faith.*

Forest Causes' to make an impassioned two-hour speech (also at Brigstock) in front of a restless agitated crowd. He spoke, not about forest affairs but about monarchs of the past century, during which he slandered the Protestant Edward VI and Elizabeth and stated his admiration for Catholic Mary. Needless to say, after a judicial inquiry he was forced to resign his position.

Strange things have also been uncovered in county churches. Underfloor atmospheric conditions can be conducive to maintaining an outstanding state of preservation of whatever is buried and sealed in. Whilst levering up the uneven flagstones of the floor of the Church of All Saints at Rushton in 1869, to make the floor more level, workmen discovered a large area filled with charcoal. Carefully agitating the contents, they were astonished to find a woman's body, with all its features intact, as if she had just been buried. They were even more astounded when after a few minutes of exposure to the air, the body completely disintegrated. Little else is known, and theories abounded as to who she was or when she was buried, until the incident vanished from memory. It is possible that the burial was of a very early date, probably from a much earlier church on that site. In late Saxon times, charcoal was used in higher status burials, to ensure, according to popular belief (but not in theological teachings), that the body was in a pure, complete form, ready to 'rise again'. More fortunate, however, was another exhumed body. In 1930, whilst making improvements to the heating system at the Church of St Edmund at Warkton, a coffin was unearthed. It contained the perfectly preserved body of a young female with long hair, which had been buried at some time during the sixteenth century. It was subsequently resealed and reinterred at the same spot.

The county is well known for its saints, St Werburga, St Rumbold, St Cyneburga, St Lois/St Lucien, St Wilfred, St Pega and even St Patrick, all of whom had some kind of association with the county, however tenuous. There is another saint however, St Ragener, who is a little less familiar. He was said to have been a native of 'Hamtun' (Northampton) and was a nephew of St Edmund of East Anglia. He fought the Danish hordes, was captured by them and tortured to death for not denying Christianity. His body was taken to St Peter's at Northampton, where an ornately decorated lid for his reliquary can be seen in the church today, but it was not always there, having been used over the years variously as a door lintel for a nearby cottage and a mantelpiece in a brewery. However, it is his association with a certain, supposedly true, miracle, which took place a short time after his bones were placed in the church some time after AD 870, that will be examined here.

A young girl, Algiva of Abington, had been born hamstrung from birth and was forced to beg around the town on her hands and knees. A priest in charge at the church was passing by the market place when he spotted her and feeling a deep sense of pity, with Easter Sunday being imminent, invited her to his dwelling for food and sustenance. He told her that her infirmity might be cured if she followed a set of procedures in the church. She was first shriven and then told to spend the whole night alone in the church, at prayer. After several hours performing this duty, the whole church suddenly became illuminated with a bright light, almost like fire, and a snow white dove appeared, flying around the building excitedly. It then came towards her, and sprinkled holy water with its wings over her, whereupon she could stand up to normal height, with strength taking hold of her bones. Two bells started to ring by themselves, waking up the priest and the whole neighbourhood. As they all entered, they were amazed at the sight that confronted them and it became a talking point all round the town. The priest (officiating at the church temporarily and not knowing of St Ragener) was convinced that the reliquary contained the remains of a particularly venerable saint, and he invited a huge crowd to come along after fasting to watch the lid being removed. Among those present were large numbers of sick and infirm townsfolk, eager to see what was inside and what would happen. When the lid was removed, a vast out-flowing of goodness swept through everyone. Those with afflictions, like Algiva, found themselves cured. Word subsequently spread around the region, and for many years afterwards other people with ailments would come to the church at the time of its patronal feast in the hope of a repeat miracle.

The above tale, like many other saints' tales, is supposed to have been based on real-life events. However, the following 'miracles' definitely *never* happened. In 1301, John, the Archdeacon of Northampton, issued a letter to all churches in the Archdeaconry, forbidding pilgrimages to 'Cherleton' (East Carlton):

> It has come to our hearing that some of unstable faith, flock together from different areas to the chapel of Cherleton by reason of feigned pilgrimage there because by the rewards of certain people who just like common robbers, and not caring for the other chapel [? the wording here is unclear] in the same church, in the year now unfolded, to have been caught and one having been killed by them from those pursuing the same [thing] in the same chapel, they were given up with a last entreaty outside the same... Alleging there to be miracles of healing they reverence the same place with offerings of animals, and in other ways in the manner of pagans, and this done by the inhabitants of the town of Cherleton who receive the offerings and use them for their own benefit, as is said they are rashly persuaded...

He then goes on to tell all priests to stress, during every Sunday Mass, that anyone going on such a pilgrimage would be excommunicated and asks them to punish any such offenders in any manner they saw fit! And, that those villagers of East Carlton who had received offerings were to appear before the hierarchy and receive appropriate justice. The nature of the miracles is not mentioned, but the incident shows the gullibility of our ancestors – perhaps the pilgrimages were an early, more primitive form of winning the lottery!

Continuing with a 'religious' theme, the ghostly monk that appears on the road between Corby and Kettering, although not believed by everyone as genuine, has some basis in fact but only in so far as that, an unknown to many people, monks *did* walk from nearby Pipewell Abbey to take services in three local churches: Great Oakley, Barford and Great Newton. Significantly, the walk to the latter settlement would have crossed the road where the supposed apparition is seen, and Barford, which no longer exists (one of the seventy plus deserted medieval villages of the county), lay close by. What is more intriguing, however, is that on one fine summer evening at nearby Rushton, a minister had just finished clearing up after a service in the Church of All Saints and decided to go for a quick walk along the track almost opposite the church towards Pipewell when he was startled by a 'nebulous' procession of monks coming towards him – a one-off experience he has never forgotten.

Just as uncanny are those houses around the county that have a room which always seems either hot or cold, no matter what the weather or season. Similarly, there are tales of a smell of tobacco in a house where no one smokes. The most amazing situation, however, occurs now and again at a house in Stanion with a religious connection – possibly a former priest's dwelling, judging by one of its architectural features and its proximity to the church. On Fridays, there can be a distinct smell of fish inside the house, with no obvious provenance. One can only speculate.

PEOPLE AND EVENTS

The county has witnessed some tragic events, amazing feats and interesting characters throughout its history. One of these is an event that was of great importance and seriousness, affecting three counties but with echoes elsewhere, and yet until recently was consigned to oblivion and known by only a few scholars and devotees of social history. This was the Midlands Revolt of 1607.

The actions of greedy landowners had led to many peasants being deprived of their dwellings, livelihoods and common rights, leaving them to wander in a state of poverty and misery with their families. This was due to the enclosure of land, a process that had been going on since the years following the Black Death in the fourteenth century. This was a process whereby landowners began to convert their land from arable to pasture, dividing large open stretches into smaller, hedged off units for the use of sheep, whose wool was highly prized in Europe and fetched attractive high prices – and, unlike peasants, did not need payment. By the end of the sixteenth century, there had been significant economic and demographic changes, leading to an increase in population and pressure on the land for food crops, not helped by export of grain to Europe, which in turn led to high prices and shortages.

Among the landowners were the heads of two branches of the Tresham family, two cousins, both confusingly named 'Sir Thomas', one of whom was based at Rushton and the other, at Newton. The former had begun enclosing his land at Haselbech, Pytchley and Rushton, and also had his sights set on Orton, near Rothwell. Another place targeted was Great Houghton, a village that could have been destroyed if enclosure had gone ahead; the other cousin, more questionably, began building a lodge and dividing up land near Little Oakley and Geddington Woods, known as The Brand, that he claimed was within Newton parish but was actually land where the villagers of Geddington, Stanion, and Little Oakley exercised their common rights.

Marks made by the Newton rebels at Boughton House in 1607.

A large contingent of peasants, together with sympathetic tradesmen and artisans, calling themselves The Levellers (not to be confused with the disaffected Parliamentary troops of the same name in later years) began tearing up and breaking down the landowners' work, initially in Warwickshire and Leicestershire. The group was led by John Reynolds, alias 'Captain Pouch', so-called for the leather bag he wore, supposedly containing a protective 'charm against all-comers' (which later turned out to be a piece of mouldy green cheese), and who boasted divine sanction for their mission. Prior to their arrival in Northamptonshire, however, he was arrested and so did not take part in the tragedy that was to occur at Newton on 8 June that year.

Around a thousand protesters – men, women and children – gathered at The Brand with simple tools and makeshift weapons, their ranks swollen with people from nearby villages and towns. Whilst levelling the area, the militia arrived, summoned by Sir Anthony Mildmay of Apethorpe Hall. After a lengthy confrontation, over forty levellers had been slain and a fair number wounded. In September, 143 survivors from fifteen local 'townships' had to make their mark on a document confessing to 'their heinous crimes' and 'late seditious insurrection and rebellion upon pretence of depopulation and unlawful enclosure' which led to them being 'magnanimously' pardoned by James I – except for the ringleaders who were duly hanged, drawn and quartered, their remains subsequently displayed at Thrapston, Oundle and Northampton as a deterrent to any more would-be insurgents.

It was not until the summer of 2008, after a series of yearly events and widespread publicity, that a special weekend series of events to mark the 400th anniversary of the Midlands Revolt was held at Newton, attracting a lot of visitors and interest (including a special Captain Pouch ale!). In the autumn, the tragedy finally had a more permanent form of recognition with the unveiling of a commemorative stone, set up by the Friends outside the former Church of St Faith (now a field centre) at Newton.

The memorial commemorating the 400th anniversary of the rebellion, at St Faith's, Newton.

The mystery remains, however, as to what happened to the bodies of the slain. There is no evidence of burial in local parish registers, where records even exist (despite the 1538 order that all parishes had to keep records), for the earliest surviving parish records for any of the seven nearby villages that had participated in the encounter, are those for Weekley (1550) and Warkton (1559), the others being Stanion, Newton, Geddington, Little Oakley, Corby and the town of Kettering, whose records all date much later, after 1636. Not far away, on the boundary between Geddington and Weekley, is the site of Heathen Ash, recorded in the early medieval period, and adjoining The Brand itself is Newton Spinney, which, unlike neighbouring woods, always seems to have an eerie atmosphere about it as crows nest there in large numbers, forever encircling the treetops above and raucously announcing their presence. There is a distinct possibility that this is where the bodies were taken for convenience and expediency. We will never know.

Recusancy was a widespread problem, particularly during the reign of Elizabeth I when, once again, Thomas Tresham enters the picture. The hermitage near Brampton Ash was a centre of pilgrimage for the lame and blind seeking a cure for their afflictions. The last hermit had been removed by Simon of Norwich, a staunch Catholic, and the place subsequently became 'a den of Popery'. In April 1576, Henry of Corby, a Protestant, staunch anti-Catholic and informer against recusants, was attacked with 'mighty blows of

The spinney adjoining the Brand where the Newton rebellion took place.

a crabtree cudgel' at Kettering market by Simon, who was his nephew. (It was the second drubbing he had received in three years, the first was on leaving a barber's shop in Bedford, inflicted by other aggrieved recusants.) The case was taken to the Star Chamber, where those also implicated were Tresham, Edward Norwich, and servants of Lord Mordaunt of Drayton, all armed with swords, daggers, long-spiked staves and cudgels. Sir Thomas admitted drawing his sword – but only to avoid a breach of the peace! Edward swore that his sword had got stuck when he tried to draw it out. Henry alleged that Simon had never been to church since the queen ascended the throne. Protestant witnesses gave evidence that Simon had been harbouring 'four old Catholic priests' in livery of blue and red at the hermitage, where there was also an altar, Mass book, chalice and other illegal items. Henry won the case, and Simon was duly sent to two notorious London prisons 'for popery', firstly to Fleet and secondly, in November 1578, to Marshalsea, where he gained his freedom five years later, but Tresham and the others were fortunate to be acquitted.

Nonconformists also suffered until the 1689 Toleration Act granting them freedom of worship (except Catholics and Quakers), subject to certain

The former chapel of the Nonconformists at Ashley, c.1890.

conditions which obliged them to register their place of worship and forbade them to meet in dwellings. Even after this Act, some Nonconformists suffered, especially those at Ashley, who met in a barn adjoining a farmhouse at Westhorp, which acted as a place of worship for thirteen local villages. The group met in complete darkness, and looked up the chimney at the end of a long session to see if dawn was breaking – they even had lookouts at strategic places for any officials that might be heading their way, such measures being taken perhaps because they had not followed the official line mentioned above. In 1717 the local rector felt so strongly about Nonconformism in his parish that he called out the militia to set fire to the building! Thereafter, the group carried firearms to protect their chapel. Things seem to have settled down, and in 1831 land was bought for a burial ground and the Manse built for their minister.

During the Second World War, at a time when Britain was being subjected to continuous bombing by the Luftwaffe, ten German Dornier bombers were heading towards Derby when one was hit by a British Defiant aircraft patrolling over the Weldon area at the time. It quickly crashed to the ground, just south of the village, damaging a farmhouse and causing shock to those within – the same house being hit, coincidentally, during the First World War by a Zeppelin unloading its bombs. An RAF team had the difficult task of clearing a large area where the debris had been scattered. It was recorded that five bodies of the crew had been recovered and that some of the bomb load had been found unexploded. These were dealt with the following Sunday morning, after householders had been warned to leave their windows open to avoid blast damage. Unofficially, several villagers helped the recovery team by stealthily collecting souvenirs which were displayed after the war at an aviation exhibition held at Wicksteed Park, in Kettering. One person found an airman's boot but quickly returned it, after he had found part of a foot in it.

At a funeral service conducted at the village church of St Mary the following week, the five coffins were lowered side by side into a common grave and covered with a German flag. Initially there was only one grave marker with the name of the aircraft's captain; the others bore a cross with the words: 'an unknown German airman'. After the war, three of the names were added, but the fifth marker remained as it was, until 1963 when all five were disinterred with due ceremony and buried at the German Military Cemetery at Cannock Chase, where they still remain today. However, speculation as to the identity of the fifth crewmember continued long afterwards, just as many people in the village still insist today (contrary to the facts) that Rudolph Hesse was often seen under escort at a house overlooking a green on the road to Corby. Not even the official records in Germany have solved the mystery. Normally this type of plane would have had a four-man crew, and the most likely conclusion, therefore, is that as the plane was flying low (600ft), unlike its companions, and he was one of a number of spies being parachuted into the county at the time. The reverse was happening at nearby Harrington airfield, where the British Special Operations Executive was organising and flying secret missions (Operation Carpetbagger) for dropping agents, propaganda, weapons and supplies to resistance groups in occupied Europe.

The northern area of the county, with its large stretches of flat land, saw the construction of several airbases – mainly for the USAAF – to fly bombers, fighters and carriers to Europe, beginning in the summer of 1942 and lasting almost three years. The remains of the long straight landing strips, slip roads and crumbling buildings can still be seen today, ghosts of a dramatic era when well over 500 aircraft were lost and over 1,500 personnel perished. It is said that coins of the period embedded in the beams of the bar at the Vane Arms, Sudborough, one of several hostelries patronised by US airforce personnel at the time, are those of men who flew out on a mission from nearby Grafton Underwood airfield but never returned. Prior to flying, a coin would customarily be slotted into one of the cracks, and those lucky to come back safely took out their coin when visiting the pub again. In the vicinity of another

A group of USAAF airmen at the Kingscliffe airbase, 1944.

base, at Kingscliffe, there are cases of some women drivers still refusing to use the road at night after having had, or heard about, unnerving experiences in the vicinity of the airfield.

This airfield was noteworthy in two other ways. When an outbreak of scurvy hit the area, US personnel donated crates of oranges to the children of the village. They were so generous, however, that there was a surfeit of crates and other villages benefitted from this gesture of goodwill. The second notable event was that the renowned US bandleader, Glenn Miller, played his last ever airfield hangar concert there on 4 October 1944. Just over two months later, on 15 December, whilst en route to a concert in France, his plane disappeared whilst flying over the Channel. A memorial commemorating the concert can be seen on the concrete base of the former hanger at the far side of the airfield, not far from the road between Apethorpe and Nassington.

Another celebrity was based at Polebrook airfield and had a private room for entertaining at the Old Three Cocks in Brigstock. His name was Clark Gable. One former barmaid who served him regularly has vivid memories of those times, one of which was being given a pound note signed by him which

The monument to Glenn Miller on the site of the former aircraft hangar at Kingscliffe.

she kept for years afterwards. The other memory, which would have made her the envy of many star-struck girls of the time, was when he took her to the Odeon cinema in nearby Kettering to watch his most famous film, *Gone With The Wind*!

Going back in time to the seventeenth century, there are many well-documented cases of 'witchcraft' in the county, the most famous being those recorded at the 1612 trials in Northampton, where five so-called witches (in reality innocent, deluded people), two from Guilsborough and one each from Raunds, Thrapston and Stanwick, were found guilty and hanged. However, there are two less-known cases that few have heard about, records of which were hidden away until very recently and can now be found at the Northamptonshire Record Office.

The first concerns Em Napper of Scaldwell who persuaded a gullible neighbour, Elizabeth Sharpe, to steal various goods from her master. However, whilst carrying out the deed her conscience got the better of her and she confessed her misdemeanour to him, which led to Napper cursing her. Within a fortnight the curse seems to have worked when she began to suffer from a temporary loss of hearing and sight and the use of her limbs. At a subsequent arraignment in 1628, Napper was said to have made another villager lame,

An isolated group of laurel bushes within Mounterley Wood adjoining the site of a Romano-British shrine near Brigstock. This may well have been where foliage was taken for rituals. As late as the twentieth century foliage was gathered for other customs in the village.

made cheese go bad and to have had a cat-like creature follow her around. The second case was brought before court in 1632 and involved Joane Craduck, who was active around her village of Maidwell and nearby Oxendon. She had threatened a man named Richard Dalbie, to whom she was attracted but who was involved with another woman whom he was going to marry. She made a threat that there would be consequences if he did marry, which came to fruition when, after a period of languishing, he died. Like all unpopular people of the time, other trumped up charges were brought against her, including those of other local 'victims' feeling unwell after being touched by her.

In 1999, a time capsule was discovered at the Church of St John the Baptist in old Corby village. It had been inserted in the corner stone of the new north aisle after foundations were laid in 1901. To mark the end of the millennium, it was decided to open the capsule and replace it with another for future generations to discover. An opening ceremony took place on 9 September 1999, but the contents had suffered from dampness and were virtually destroyed;

An archaeological mystery at Rushton, excavated in 2005.

they included picture of the monarch, coins of the realm and a copy of the church magazine of the time. However, these were put on show, alongside two new capsules and contents reflecting our time, which were later buried inside the church after a special service.

Some spectacular archaeological finds have been made in the county over the years (many as a result of either quarrying for ironstone and gravel, or construction work) such as a gold Anglo-Saxon necklace with garnet pendants and thirty-seven beads, unearthed in 1876 at Desborough, and a well-preserved Iron Age mirror (one of only seventeen of its type found in Britain) in 1908 in the same town. Recently, on farmland in Rushton, after a few seasons excavating a Roman bathhouse and adjoining Saxon burial site, a strange structure, as yet unexplained by experts and not made public, was discovered on the periphery of the site. It consists of a set of upward-pointing timbers, set roughly in a rectangular arrangement. Another unusual find was near Brigstock, sometime between 1956 and 1970. A sacred site was uncovered, consisting of an early penannular ditch (indicative of a prehistoric timber temple) overlaid by the remains of a shrine in the form of a twelve-sided polygon, to the north of which was yet another shrine, circular in shape. Among the many associated

The hoop of a May garland from the 1950s on the Wishing Tree at Old Sulehay Woods.

finds were three pairs of equestrian statues, several votive metal 'leaf blades' (possibly for a cult official's head-dress) and six extremely rare pole tips from which rattles would be hung, together with a ferrule, for a ceremonial sceptre. Such sites also acted a stopping points for trading missions, which would leave an offering in order to get a form of 'protection' from an associated deity, for the onward journey. It is thought in some quarters that this site and nearby Collyweston, where there was a similar complex, were part of a prehistoric 'gold route' which began in the Wicklow Mountains of Ireland (which had some of the finest gold to be found) and continued overland towards the Norfolk coast, where it would be shipped to Europe.

There have been some remarkable trees in the county, many of which have succumbed to time and the elements, one of which was the Lowick Oak, which could hold a table and two chairs for dinner! One survivor, however, stands in Old Sulehay Woods near Yarwell, a large stretch of ancient woodland, within which are some remarkable trees with contorted shapes. One of these was formerly known as The Wishing Tree, a coppiced oak with seven protruding branches and a base which can seat one or two people. Inevitably, these unique features fired the imagination of local people, who believed the tree had magical properties and could grant wishes. Later, it was the destination of children from the village school, who after carrying the garland from house to house on May Day would place it on one of the boughs. The wicker hoop of one of these can still be seen today.

The forces of nature have contributed to the damage or destruction of many church spires in the county, with at least nineteen churches having been struck by lightning at one time. Some have been unlucky to have been hit more than once, like those at Raunds (four times: 1824, 1836, 1841 and 1895), Middleton Cheney (three times), Kettering and Desborough (twice). The strike at Great Billing on 11 April 1759 was recorded as follows:

> Some of the stones were whirled into the air with such an astonishing force and rapidity as to be carried a considerable distance. Many pews splintered into small pieces. The sulphurous smell was so powerful that scarcely anybody could bear to go near the church...

The community attributed the cause of the destruction and its aftermath to the Devil and the church was later rededicated as a result. A local tradition also grew up around another church, that of St Mary at Weldon, which has a lantern tower whose light is said to have guided medieval wayfarers travelling through the northern stretches of Rockingham Forest. Unfortunately, this can be disproved as, firstly, the 'forest' was not heavily wooded (according to contemporary descriptions and later maps) and, secondly, until a great storm in the nineteenth century the church had a spire, which was not rebuilt but replaced instead with a fine, small castellated octagonal lantern tower when the church was restored in 1854. This was later replaced by another lantern 'tower' in the form of a wooden cupola with glazed side panels and resembles a lighthouse lantern, and it is still lit regularly today. Strangely enough, there *are* naval connections – both associated with Horatio Nelson – in the form of two windows inside the church. One was donated by a former rector who had been given it as a gift by William Hamilton, husband of Nelson's mistress, Emma, and the other was donated by John Clarke, an assistant to a ship's surgeon in Nelson's fleet, who retired to the village at the age of twenty-five!

Other spires have not been so lucky. That at Rothwell fell down during a Sunday service on 30 September 1750 when an earthquake shook the area. The vicar duly recorded his fears in the parish register, stating 'I thought the Roof would crash then, or we would be swallowed up by the earth...' Like many others in the county it was never replaced. Worse still was that at Clopton, which was destroyed not by nature but blown up by human hands because destruction was cheaper than repair!

A house at Harringworth with medieval religious connections.

At Harringworth, across the street from the Church of St John the Baptist, there is a thatched cottage, one half of which is constructed in ironstone, the other half in limestone. It has an inner door, above which is the stonework of a medieval archway of a building with a former religious connection. It is said by some to have been a hermitage but is possibly one of two chapels recorded in the village before the Reformation. Whatever the case, a retired stockman who lived in one half of the cottage during the latter years of the last century was continually digging up bones in the garden, probably those of the religious devotees who had lived there. Visitors would sometimes be surprised to see the perfectly sound and secure door of the archway quietly open by itself for no apparent reason, even on a calm, windless day, or at night. The cause has never been satisfactorily explained.

Not so pleasant is a custom which took place in the eighteenth century at Geddington. David Townsend, the village blacksmith, published a short-lived (seven issue) magazine, *Sparks from Vulcan's Forge or Odds, Ends and Particulars; a Manuscript Periodical*, which contained an item about an 'ancient custom' that had once taken place in the village annually on Easter Monday:

The Eleanor Cross at Geddington where squirrel pelting took place in the eighteenth century

It was customary to catch squirrels in Geddington Chase and turn them loose near the Cross. The squirrels endeavouring to escape, would run up the slopes and the people would pelt them with stones, as the poor little creatures ran in and out of the stonework, trying to hide from their enemies...

David Townsend was a remarkable man in many respects. He had been born in Grafton Underwood in 1807, and after an apprenticeship he moved to Little Oakley where he and his father ran a smithy. He later transferred to Geddington where he ran the smithy opposite the Eleanor Cross. He was a staunch Nonconformist and a great advocate of temperance (after signing a pledge in 1859), which he avidly promoted around the streets of Kettering, in later years often carrying a board along the High Street advertising an important meeting. He would be seen around the streets of the town, hawking various leaflets and booklets he had had printed on this theme and other subjects, such as The Dun Cow's Rib in Stanion Church' and 'Heroes of Kettering'. He also played the fiddle and dressed in old-fashioned clothing, such as a long-sleeved waistcoat, tight breeches, worsted stockings and a soft cap with a turndown flap (tied by a ribbon and attached to the ear-tabs on top of his head). He also visited villages like Rushton where he took a 'mysterious' round tin containing bullseyes, and these he would hand out, whilst telling jokes, to schoolchildren. Always a great believer in education for the masses, there was an incident in his earlier days at Geddington where he met a strong adversary in the form of the abrasive anti-nonconformist vicar, aptly named William Church. (The same man would later argue with the lord of the manor of Great Oakley, Sir Arthur de Capell Brooke – a former explorer and a founder member of the Raleigh Society, which later evolved into the Royal Geographical Society – who had defended an open-air service held in Geddington in 1856. Church sent a strong letter to him full of objections, which was countered with an equally strong argument that made the vicar back down.)

When Townsend opened an evening school in 1849 to give the children of the village some extra education, Church objected to a 'dissenter' teaching his Sunday school attendees and threatened the parents with the exclusion of their children from Sunday school. It had the desired effect and some were immediately withdrawn. This led to Townsend holding a public meeting and publishing the speech he made at the event, urging parents to stand up to the bullying tactics of the vicar, but this was to no avail and the school closed.

After moving to Kettering, he was more successful with his publications, amongst which was the book *The Gipsies of Northamptonshire*, a valuable, and now extremely scarce, historical document in verse form. It was published in 1877, and describes the gypsy way of life as it was fifty years earlier in great detail – a bygone age in an era of great change, with enclosure and turnpike roads altering the face of the landscape and centuries of tradition and a set lifestyle. His first encounters with them were during his childhood at Grafton Underwood. In the preface to the book, he recalls:

At the village feast I used to go with my brother and sister to the village and at such times, one or two Gipsy men with violins, and a female with a tambourine used to go from door to door all round the village and play upon their instruments, and if there happened to be young people at any of the houses, those young people would dance to the music. The Gipsies got well paid for these musical performances, both in ale and plum pudding, and money. They kept up the practice all the afternoon at feast times and I, with many children used to follow them from door to door to hear the music. In the evening, some of the farmers would engage them to play at a private party, whilst others would be engaged at an alehouse, or some cottage, to play for dancing among young people of the working class. The sort of music they used to play were hornpipes, reels and country dances.

He later learnt much more about their way of life, as a young man working at Little Oakley, where they helped him learn to play the fiddle (like the county poet, John Clare, had done when the gipsies visited Helpston). He describes them as travelling in groups of two or three, but as many as fifty in the summer, 'together with horses, donkeys, dogs, jackdaws, jays and bantam cocks'. Their furniture would be transported by hanging it on each side of one donkey, with bedding and tent material on another, whilst babies were carried on their mothers' backs. They would set up their camps in the form of simple tents, consisting of 'two rows of rods stuck in the ground, which met at the top', and which were encircled with blankets on the outside. Breakfast would often be rabbit stew, and for other meals they were adept at quickly preparing a freshly-caught hare or hedgehog (a delicacy) by spreading the carcass 'quite flat, then sticking a skewer across it', roasting the latter 'with the bristles on'. They disliked tramps, calling them 'hedge creepers'. Visitors, however, were always welcome to join them for conversation or a smoke, whilst sitting cross-legged on the floor. He describes them as having as 'dark eyes, very dark flowing hair – often over their shoulders – and the men as always being clean-shaven 'as clean as a new pin'. Everyday clothing was 'old, of mean appearance and none too clean' but their 'holiday' dress, was very special: the younger women wearing white and coloured ribbon round the waist with 'a monstrous bow', and lace and jewels 'bedecking bosom, breast and neck'. They rarely wore bonnets, preferring a handkerchief to cover their hair. The men would wear large silver buckles on their shoes with clean white stockings, and breeches buttoned at the knees, and they wore a 'soft coat with buttons as big as half a crown'.

He soon got on friendly terms with one group that regularly camped along a track on the edge of the village, and describes how they would come to the village to beg straw from the farmers for their donkeys, and to get the animals shod at his smithy, where he would also make new sets of screws for the tambourines of their women. In general, there appears to have been little distrust of the gypsies by the villagers – in contrast to what would happen in later years in most places.

Gypsy women, of course, have always been noted for their habit of telling fortunes. Townsend looks at one such occasion, perhaps fictitious but certainly based on reality, with a touch of humour, as one gullible villager succumbs to having her palm read by a gypsy woman selling goods from door to door, usually skilfully hand-made items of woodwork such as pegs or a basket:

Sukey once had her fortune told
When she was getting rather old
Because she was not satisfied
That Joe would take her for his bride,
She also thought Joe did not seem
To love so much as she loved him.
One day a Gipsy woman came
To Sukey's door (a keen old dame),
To try to sell a cabbage net,
Or beg whatever she could get.
And Sukey was at home alone,
And so she said in gentle tone –
'Mistress, if I may be so bold,
I want to have my fortune told.'
'O yes, my dear, God bless thee, child.'
The Gipsy woman said and smiled,
'You are in love, you will feel dull
Until the moon is in the full,
But when she shows her mystic light
You very soon will be alright.'

Festive occasions, such as fairs, were also a time that gypsies took advantage of. Townsend describes two forms of entertainment laid on by them, one similar to roulette:

They had a horizontal wheel
Upon a pivot made of steel,
And just beyond its outer edge
A marble ran round on a ledge,
Equally swift in rapid play
The wheel went round contrary way;
All round the wheel, on the top side,
Were small recesses one inch wide,
And into which the marble went
When all its force was nearly spent;
And when it could no longer run,
There it remained, the game was done.
On this machine, the rustic clown
Would often put his half-pence down,

And stand with smiling harmless grin
To see the Gipsy woman win.
There also was another stall
Prepared to meet the wants of all;
At this some ancient withered hag
Had tickets in a 'lucky bag',
A bag perhaps eight inches square
And very rough indeed with hair,
It might be made of silk within,
But rough outside with hairy skin;
Such folks as were extremely raw
Would pay a penny and then draw
A ticket from this lucky place,
And get a farthing bodkin case.

David Townsend, who boasted that he lived under three different monarchs, died at the ripe old age of eighty-nine. He is now long forgotten but deserves an honoured place in the annals of the county's history.

Abner Brown, scholar and vicar of Pytchley (1832-1851) and Gretton (1851-1872), was another who wrote about the habits of gypsies, his description determined partly by scholarship and partly from local observation:

They prefer a quiet churchyard with a handsome coffin, as opposed to public ceremony... they have a great desire to have their children christened. They hold the Buddhist doctrine of transmigration of the soul...They will pay a sexton yearly to have all their family graves kept up. There are favourite churchyards amongst them...their dead are carried long distances to those churchyards...

He also wrote other snippets of local information and folklore, such as village May Day customs and a cleft willow tree through which superstitious local people used to pass their sick children in the hope of a cure:

An ancient cleft willow, half a mile down the lane leading northwards from Pytchley was used as a stile. Once famous for curing diseased children who were pushed through the cleft, even while the opening was small. There are still living at Pytchley persons whose parents and grandparents had in their infancy gone through this Druidical process.

THE GIPSIES

OF

NORTHAMPTONSHIRE:

THEIR MANNER OF LIFE,

FESTIVE AMUSEMENTS, AND FORTUNE TELLING,

FIFTY YEARS AGO,

BY

DAVID TOWNSEND,

OF KETTERING.

This is the book that you should buy,
And if you ask the reason why,
The answer is, it tells you more
Than you have ever read before.

KETTERING: J. H. WADDINGTON, PRINTER, HIGH STREET.
1877.

The title page to David Townsend's rare book on the lifestyle of gypsies in the county.

Just as intriguing are his references to local will o' the wisps, which, like glow worms, are an uncommon sight today, having become casualties of modern land management:

> The moist alluvial meadows between Gretton and the sluggish river Welland lately abounded with the *ignis fatuus*, six or eight lights having been occasionally seen at once within the space of half a mile square, but the extensive drainings of the last few years have almost banished this beautiful and freakish night ornament of our landscape.

He also describes a 'singular incident' which occurred following a funeral after a dark stormy afternoon when he was the incumbent of the church at Pytchley:

> Returning home at night after visiting a sick person in the village, and passing along the lonely path through the churchyard, which is surrounded by trees, I was surprised to perceive a pale haze in the corner of it, and going up the path lined with wet leaves which the gusts of wind shook, and then up to the light, I saw a number of strange-looking blue gleams, larger than candles, over the newly-made graves. It was too dark to avoid stumbling over the graves and I could not make out those silent, still and spectre-like dead-lights or corpse candles, until I grasped one and found my own hand covered with blue light... They were pieces of decayed coffin shield brought into the air while their phosphorus was in a state to disengage itself. This spoilt a great ghost story or fairy tale.

These were notes accompanying a rare book which contained a collection of verse, *Lyrical Pieces* (published in London in 1869), consisting of 255 poems, mainly composed by his daughter Anne (1834-1858). Anne was a talented girl, who tragically died at the young age of twenty-four whilst nursing the sick during an epidemic. Her father wrote:

> The dates of her compositions range from childhood to the close of her life, but chiefly between the ages of twelve and twenty. Fond of poetry from her earliest years, she was wont to compose different poems and fragments upon the same subject, and to make repeated versions of the same poem. Some of her verses have only been known to her friends since her death. Affection recognises in her poetry, besides more sacred features of her character, her intense love of nature, and her sunny, genial freshness of idea. Like other children, she delighted also to sport

LYRICAL PIECES,

SECULAR AND SACRED,

FROM THE HOME CIRCLE OF A COUNTRY PARSONAGE.

With numerous Illustrative Vignettes,

AND WITH ARCHÆOLOGICAL AND OTHER NOTES.

Spes laeta, spes lucis aeternae.

EDITED BY

ABNER W. BROWN, M.A.,

VICAR OF GRETTON, NORTHAMPTONSHIRE; AND HONORARY CANON OF
PETERBOROUGH.

London:

SAMPSON LOW, SON & MARSTON.

1869.

The title page to Abner Brown's book of verse by his daughter, Anne, 1869.

with the wild creations of fairy mythology; that imaginary world of beautiful phantasms, which, in so far as it is a genuine belief, owes its origin to ignorance of natural phenomena...

Starting at an early age, she usually dated each poem, providing a pointer to how her style would flower and mature over the years. One of her earliest efforts, at the age of eight, was about the death of a pet canary, whilst later efforts gave reign to her vivid imagination with a set of colourful fairy poems. Others reflected her love of the countryside, one of which was a precursor of today's concerns about the environment, in which she gives an old endangered lime tree a voice against its threatened destruction at a time Pytchley Hall, in whose grounds it stood, was scheduled to be demolished, and a new roadway planned in the vicinity. Here is an edited version of the original thirteen-verse poem:

Ah ruthless lord of my unhappy fate!
How may I move thy hand to stay thy steel?
How to win thy heart to pause, ere yet too late,
And hear my woodland groans, my anguish feel?

Beneath my widespread arms in childhood played,
The patriarchs of the village, old and gray,
And now their children's children seek my shade,
And shake their golden ringlets as they play.
Dread of my fall with terror overwhelm
Those groves whose finish I was made to be
That long-sequestered avenue of elms
Whose leafy grandeur leads to nought but me.

The lordly sycamores all, all are gone
And must the lime tree really, really fall?
Is its bright life for ever, o'er and done?
The relic last of barons' ancient hall.

Among her earliest efforts was 'The Child's Song in the Copse', composed when she was twelve years old, already showing her affection for the natural landscape of the county:

How pleasant 'tis to wander in the low coppice wood
And 'mid the trees to ponder, on everything that's good!

To look towards the sky, on a bright summer's day
And watch with half-shut eye, the sweet lark's airy way.

To pluck the ivy green, from off the old oak tree,
And in the fair wild scene, for many an hour to be.

One of her most evocative poems is 'Summer Night In The Forest', where she combines several of her favourite motifs, which recur frequently elsewhere in her work and which encapsulate a world once familiar in the county (with creatures and birds such as the landrail – or corncrake - referred to in the eighth verse, which was well-known in the county at one time for 'singing' throughout the summer) but a which is now slowly disappearing:

Cool and sweet is August's night,
'Mid the forest's riding deep;
When the dewy moonbeams white,
Quivering through the branches weep.

Balmy perfumes – basil, thyme,
Woodbine, roses, eglantine;
Lovely wood-sage, flowery lime,
Mix sweet scents with resin-pine.
Save that yonder night-shade rank
Hot deceitful odour streams;
Or the boggy pond-weed dank
Warns where *ignis fatuus* gleams.

Cheering glow worms, nature's boon,
Sparkle round like diamonds bright;
Drops from the resplendent moon,
Spilled as 'twere – of silvery light!

Velvet winged the owl sails past,
Seeming from the ground to rise;
Flashing like a spirit fast,
Soft and noiselessly it flies.

Field mice creep among the grass,
Weasels hunt their lively prey;

Noisy mallards rushing, pass,
Rabbits gambol in the Way.

Droning beetles, unseen, hum;
Strangely-jarring night-hawks cry;
Flittering bats incessant come;
Snowy ghost-moths dazzle by.

Hushed the nightingale's sweet lay
Lonely sounds the reed-wren's song;
Plovers whistle far away,
Plaining landrails murmur long.

Man's whole world of hope and fear
Lies at rest in silent sleep;
All alone with nature here,
We our placid vigil keep.

Softly sweet is all the air,
Peaceful its delicious balm;
Nought awakens weary care:
'Tis not sleep, but blessed calm.
Skies and stars are all awake;
Nature's powers their work all ply;
And the Hand which did us make,
Guards us with unslumbering eye.

Like David Townsend, the Wellingborough shoemaker and poet, John Askham also regretted and deplored the changes to the traditional way of life in the county taking place during the nineteenth century. In his 1893 'Sketches in Prose and Verse', he sums this up perfectly:

The hand of change is on everything. It collars our old institutions and with the rudest grip, shakes the life out of them in no time, and so metamorphoses them, that we can hardly recognise them.

Among those 'institutions' under threat at the time were tollgates, which in his eyes were 'another national bulwark'. He wallows in nostalgia, as he recreates some of the journeys he once made, especially when he would pass through them in carriers' carts, which 'the young whipper snappers of today would turn their noses up at riding from Wellingborough to Northampton in'. He describes the colour and the hive of activity where they stood:

> The toll-gates were to us what lighthouses are to the mariner, and we hailed them as welcome omens. There was a break at the 'World's End' which meant pork pie, pigs' puddings, ale and rum-and-water...There was much to be desired in toll gate life. In addition to the regular gentle flow into the treasury, there were sudden risings... fete tides for instance, upon whose dancing waves floated all manner of large and small craft; flowers show freshets, foundation stone driblets, agricultural feeders... [and during the arrival of a fair] there was much chaffering, not to say wrangling between Wombwell [the visiting fair owner] and the toll-gater. Wombwell's arithmetic never tallied with the toll-gater's arithmetic, the latter counting more four-footed animals than the former. Loud protests were heard from royal tigers and lions at the delay; parrots entered into the conversation; bears stood on their hind leg to make enquiries...

Another clergyman scholar in the county was Talbot Keene, vicar of Brigstock for fifty-one years, who served the village church from 1773 until his death in 1824. He too published a book of poetry (*Miscellaneous Pieces: Original and Collected by a Clergyman of Northamptonshire*, 1787), although his writing is rather heavy going and somewhat pedantic for the modern reader, with frequent quotations in Latin. One piece was about the vicarage garden and his visitors! However, another poem is of special merit, recording a great oak that stood in nearby Geddington Chase, which was 'shivered to pieces' by lightning during a severe storm in June 1780, when several trees were thrown a considerable distance and a large limb of one particular tree was driven deep into the ground:

> By Jove's red Arm, high tow'ring in its pride
> The knotted oak was struck and instant died
> The limbs now scatter'd fill the groves vast plain
> The sylvan gods can scarce their lofts sustain
> Thrice happy they who born to low estate
> Fall not the victims of superior fate.

Another writer who warrants mention is Henry Kaye Bonney, 1780-1862, who was born at Tansor where his father was rector. After matriculating he was collated to the Nassington Prebend of Lincoln Cathedral and subsequently became rector of Kingscliffe in 1810. During his incumbency, he compiled an unpublished manuscript about the history of that village. One section deals at great length with the remarkable William Law (1686-1761), a renowned theologian who returned to his home village with two female acolytes who lived with him in his house. One was Elizabeth Hutcheson, a wealthy widow who founded almshouses and schools with him in the village and the other was the sister of Edward Gibbon, author of *The Decline and Fall of the Roman Empire*. He followed a set routine from which rarely wavered, breakfasting on chocolate, spending the morning in his study, eating a moderate dinner specifically on a wooden platter, then retiring to his chamber until teatime when he joined the two ladies, but eating nothing except a raisin or two, then going for a walk, followed by supper with two glasses of wine, Bible reading and prayers, then again to his chambers to smoke and drink a glass of water after which at nine o'clock, like the rest of the household, he retired to bed. Apart from this, he was a generous man to the poor, giving money, food or clothes to anyone in need. There always had to be broth in the kitchen, which he tasted for its nutritional value, and if not satisfied he would add ale, wine or ginger. He would distribute milk from his four cows with his own hands. However, word soon got around about his charity, and some better-off villagers would take advantage by going behind the church, change out of their good clothes into rags and then go to the window of his study, where they would receive new clothing:

A hand so open, and so liberal a heart might easily be subject to imposition, and numerous instances of hypocrisy are narrated, in which Persons have been known to change their better clothing, sheltered by the projecting buttresses of the church, for rags – and thus disguised, proceed to the well-known window...

In 1889, on Oak Apple Day at Werrington (now outside the county), a letter being read out to the Board of Guardians of Peterborough Workhouse led to howls of laughter from those present. It was from local man searching for wife, and was worded as follows:

Gentlemen, I was looking through some old newspapers last week and I see about a man wanting a wife out of the Union, and do the same as I am an old bachelor and I hear there are plenty of women in the big house. Let me know as soon as you can if there is one as wants a good husband, and do not care how old she is. When I see the chaps and gals in our village larfing and talking and giggling and plaing, it makes me blud run cold, and me a single chap. Let me know soon, John Michel.

In the days before photography, a worded description was the only way to give some idea of the appearance of a wanted man or woman. Sometimes these can be hilarious to modern eyes, such as that as for an accomplice of the well-known robber Huffey White, in 1813, who is described as 'looking like a Horse Dealer'! One of the most unusual 'wanted' notices the county has ever seen, was not for a common criminal, but for this 'culprit' from the village of Orlingbury, who had been missing for three years:

Absconded from his Family, July 16th, 1781. Thomas Harrison, Labourer, about 40 years of age, 5 feet 9 inches high, of a sallow Complexion, light brown Hair, crooked Nose, very slovenly in his Dress, goes clumsy and stooping his Gait. If the said Tho. Harrison will return Home and provide for his Family, within one Week after this Publication, he will be received with Kindness and due Notice taken of his just Complaints. But if he neglects his Indulgence beyond the Time offered, he will be deemed a Vagabond. 10/- Reward offered by a J.P. for anyone 'taking him up', and 5/- for recovering him to the parish of Orlingbury by the overseers or churchwardens of the parish'. [28 July 1784]

Sometimes, however, justice would be meted out without the help of the law. Such a case occurred at Wappenham in the seventeenth century, involving a colourful character, Theophilus Hart, who had somewhat dubiously been ordained a minster in the parish, after the ejection of the incumbent for failure to submit to the new Act of Uniformity in 1662. On top of this he later became vicar of Blakesley by other under-hand methods, possibly bribery. He also managed somehow to become lord of the manor, via accumulated wealth and the precarious financial position of the previous person. In this capacity, he soon made himself unpopular by bringing lawsuits against many parishioners for trivial offences. He continued to ride his luck until 1685, when the village butcher, George Terry, called at the rectory and found his wife in bed with the sixty-five year old. Hart fled naked across the fields, but the butcher, being more agile and carrying a tool of his trade, dispensed justice on the head of his quarry, putting an end to his antics forever. Despite gaining personal satisfaction, Terry was hanged for murder in May that year.

Finally, try to fathom out this little conundrum, which appeared in the *Northampton Mercury*, on 1 December 1798, describing the relationships of two Corby families:

The master and mistress of one family are both father and mother, brother and sister, to the master and mistress of the other family. Consequently, both grandfather and grandmother, and uncle and aunt to their children; while the master and mistress of the second family are both brother and sister and son and daughter to the master and mistress of the first; also uncle and aunt and cousins, at the same time to their children The mistress of the second family is sister to her own father, and aunt to her own brothers and sisters.

LOCAL PLACE NAME PRONUNCIATION

Over the centuries, both the pronunciation and spelling of place names have undergone substantial, and in some cases drastic, changes which have altered the original name beyond recognition. Notable examples of this are Stanere (Stanion), Wendleberie (Wellingborough), Cytringeham (Kettering), Liceberge (Litchborough), Wilavestone (Wilbarston), Undele (Oundle), Thingden (Finedon), Cewecumbe (Chacomb), and Navesberie (Naseby). Many of these transformations were the result of radical changes in the English language from Old English, through Middle English (c.1150-1500) and into Modern English, and even in the later period, both pre- and post-standardisation in spelling during the mid 1700s did not halt variations in how they were recorded or spoken.

Many names did become standardised across the county, especially those containing an initial 'w' in the second component of the name, which, whilst retained in the spelling, was assimilated when spoken, for example, Southwick ('suthick'), Culworth ('cullerth'). Names like Pipewell, lost the initial 'e' when spoken, but in the case of the river Nene, the county was – and still is – strongly divided as to whether it is pronounced 'neen' or 'nen'!

In many cases, however, a village or town pronounced its name in a different way than one would expect, partly from local dialect or as a result of tradition – something that could (and still can) confuse outsiders! Even within a community such as Raunds, different pronunciations of the name took root depending on which part of the town one lived. On the whole, however, much local pronunciation has gradually died out as time and demographic changes have taken their toll. The list below, whilst not exhaustive, gives some idea of the colour, flavour and range of what could once be heard in the county.

Aldwincle – Onikil
Althorp – Oltrop
Arthingworth – Ardenerth
Blisworth – Blisserth
Boughton – Buckton
Broughton – Brighton
Caldecote – Cawcut
Charwelton – Charlton
Chelveston – Cheston
Collingtree – Colentraugh
Creaton – Critton
Deenethorpe – Dingthorp, Dynthorp
Duston – Dusson
Easton Maudit – Eason Maudit
Evenly – Imly
Farthinghoe – Farnigo
Faxton – Faraxton
Heyford – Hefford
Holcot – Hocut
Holdenby – Holmby
Irthlingborough – Artleburra
Lowick – Luff(w)ick
Mears Ashby – Mares Ashby
Morehay – Moray, Morrey
Orlingbury – Orlibear
Pitsford – Pisford
Raunds – Rarnce
Rothersthorpe – Ruddestrop
Silverstone – Silston, Silson
Sulehay – Soolay
Weekley – Wickley
Yardley Gobion – Yardley Gubbins
Yarwell – Yarrel
Yelvertoft – Yellatut

BIBLIOGRAPHY

Allison, K. et al, *The Deserted Villages of Northamptonshire* (Leicester University Press, 1966)

Andrews, W., *Curious Church Customs* (1895)

Anstruther, G., *The Vaux of Harrowden* (Johns, 1953)

Askham, J., *Sketches in Prose and Verse* (NCM, 1893)

Baker, G., *History & Antiquities of the County of Northampton* (1822)

Bennett, J., *A Medieval Life – Cecilia Pennifader in Brigstock c. 1297-1344* (McGraw Hill, 1998)

   Women in the Medieval English Countryside (University of Chicago, 1987)

Beresford, J., *Diary of a Country Parson, James Woodforde 1740-1803* (Canterbury Press, 1999)

Bonney, H.K., *Historical notes on the History of Kingscliffe* (unpublished manuscript, *c*.1855)

Bridges, J., *History & Antiquities of Northamptonshire* (1721, published 1771)

Burrage, C., *The Early English Dissenters* (Cambridge, 1912)

Cox, J.C., *The English Parish Church* (1914)

   Parish Registers of England (reprinted, EP, 1974)

   Churchwardens' Accounts from the Fourteenth to the Seventeenth Century (1913)

Duffy, E., *The Stripping of the Altars* (Yale University Press, 1992)

Field, J., *English Field Names* (Davis and Charles, 1972)

   A History of English Field Names (Pearson, 1993)

Gelling, M., *Place Names in the Landscape* (Dent, 1984)

Gover, A. et al, *The Place Names of Northamptonshire* (Cambridge University Press, 1933)

Gomme, G.L. (ed.), *The Gentleman's Magazine Library: English Topography* (1896)

Hill, P., *Rockingham Forest Then and Now* (Orman, 1995)
   Rockingham Forest Revisited (Orman, 1998)
   Rockingham Forest (Tempus, 2005)
   Around Oundle and Thrapston (Tempus, 1997)
   In Search of the Green Man in Northamptonshire (Orman, 1998)
   Folklore of Northamptonshire (Tempus, 2005, History Press, 2009)
Hoskins, W.G., *The Making of the English Landscape* (Hodder & Stoughton, 1977)
Irons, A.E., *An Episcopal Visititation in 1570* (NNQ no.2, 1907-1909)
Jones, G., *Saints in the Landscape* (Tempus, 2007)
Longden, H. I., *Northants and Rutland Clergy from 1500 to 1802* (Archer & Goodman, 1938-52)
   The Visitation of the County of Northampton, 1681 (Harleian Society, 1935)
   Northamptonshire Families (Genealogical Magazine, vol 5, no.8, 1930)
   The Treshams of Newton and Wold (Taylor, 1886)
Manwood, J., *A Brefe Collection of Lawes of the Forest* (1592)
Markham, C., *The Low Side Windows of Northamptonshire Churches* (NOAS, 1908)
   The Liber Custumarum (Taylor, 1895)
Morton, J., *The Natural History of Northamptonshire* (1712)
Piggott, S., *William Stukeley, An Eighteenth Century Antiquary* (T & H, 1985)
Serjeantson, R., *A Medieval Legend of St Peter's, Northampton* (Northampton, 1907)
Taylor, J., *Antiquarian Memoranda and Biographies* (1901)
   Biblioteca Northantonensis (vols 1-71, Northampton, 1901)
Thistleton, J.F., *Church Lore Gleanings* (1892)
Thomas, K., *Religion and the Decline of Magic* (Penguin University Books, 1973)
Townsend, D., *The Gypsies of Northamptonshire* (Kettering, 1877)
Turner, G.J. (ed.), *Select Pleas of the Forest* (Selden Society, vol .XIII, 1899)
Wake, J., *The Brudenells of Deene* (Cassell, 1954)
Wilkins, D. (ed.), *Concilia* (London, 1737)

DOCUMENTS, PERIODICALS, REPORTS AND OTHER RECORDS

'The Parish Churches and Religious Houses of Northamptonshire: their Dedications, Altars, Images and Lights' (ed. J.C. Cox, in Archaeological Journal LXXX, 1913)

'The Parish Churches of Northamptonshire, temp. Henry VIII' (ed. J.C. Cox, in Archaeological Journal, XXX, 1913)

'Chantry Certificates of Northamptonshire' (Assoc. Architectural & Archaeological Reports XXXI, 1911)

Bishops' visitations, ecclesiastical court records, churchwardens' accounts, parish registers Historical Manuscripts Commission (The Montagu Papers, vols 1-3, second series, HMSO, 1926)

Alehouse Recognizances (1793-1796, 1820)

Giles Mompasson, Inn Licence Records (1617-1620)

Gay, Prof. E.F., The Midland Revolt (Transactions of the Royal Historical Society, ns. XVIII 1904)

Northamptonshire Notes & Queries, vols 1-6 (1884-1895), new series vols 1-6 (1905-1927)

Northamptonshire Past and Present (from 1948, NRS)

Northampton County Magazine (1928-1933)

Extracts from: Stamford Mercury, Northampton Mercury, Kettering Leader, Rushden Argus, The Gentleman's Magazine (from 1731 onwards)

Whellan's History, Gazetteer and Directory of Northamptonshire (1849 and 1874)

Kelly's Directories of Northamptonshire (1864-1928)

Pigot's Commercial Directory of Northamptonshire (1830)

Also available from Amberley Publishing

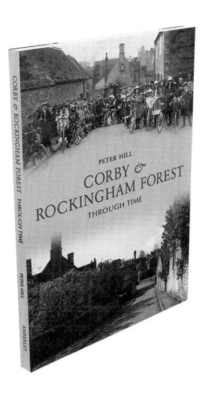

Corby & Rockingham Forest Through Time
by Peter Hill

Price: £12.99
ISBN: 978-1-84868-644-1

Available from all good bookshops or from our website
www.amberleybooks.com

Also available from Amberley Publishing

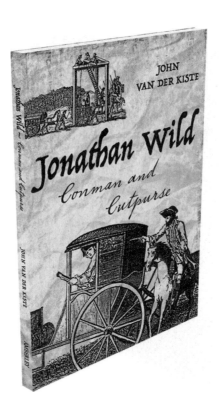

Jonathan Wild: Conman and Cutpurse
by John van der Kiste

Price: £12.99
ISBN: 978-1-84868-219-1

Available from all good bookshops or from our website
www.amberleybooks.com

Also available from Amberley Publishing

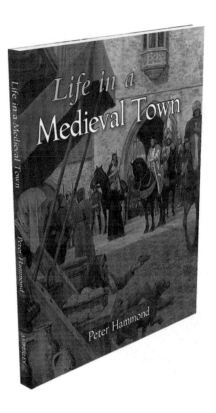

Life in a Medieval Town
by Peter Hammond

Price: £5.99
ISBN: 978-1-84868-126-2

Available from all good bookshops or from our website
www.amberleybooks.com

Also available from Amberley Publishing

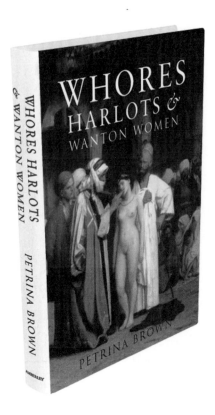

Whores, Harlots & Wanton Women
by Petrina Brown

Price: £20
ISBN: 978-1-84868-127-9

Available from all good bookshops or from our website
www.amberleybooks.com